EQUIP
for Educators

Teaching Youth (Grades 5-8) to Think and Act Responsibly

Ann-Marie DiBiase

John C. Gibbs

Granville Bud Potter

with Beth Spring

Research Press • 2612 North Mattis Avenue, Champaign, Illinois 61822
(800) 519-2707 • www.researchpress.com

Composition by Publication Services, Inc.
Cover design by Linda Brown, Positive I.D. Graphic Design
Printed by Bang Printing, Inc.

ISBN 0–87822–509–9
Library of Congress Control Number 2004115053

In memory of Arnold P. Goldstein

CONTENTS

CHAPTER 5   Equipping with Mature Moral Judgment (Social Decision Making)   123

FIGURES AND TABLES

FIGURES

TABLES

ACKNOWLEDGMENTS

We thank Janet Killens and Valerie Dunne of the District School Board of Niagara (St. Catharines, Ontario, Canada), for providing the opportunity for field testing *EQUIP for Educators*. We particularly thank Nicole Maheu for inviting *EQUIP for Educators* into her classroom and for her astute and pragmatic feedback on the program over the years. John Novak (Brock University, St. Catherines) and Douglas Clements (University of Buffalo, State University of New York) provided thoughtful advice and guidance in the development of the project and empirical research on the program. Coral Mitchell (Brock University) provided fundamental collegial support.

We also thank Karen Steiner, Dennis Wiziecki, and Jeff Helgesen at Research Press for their creativity, expertise, and patience. Research and manuscript preparation for this book were partially supported by the Social Sciences and Humanities Research Council of Canada (Internal Research Grant #336-434-046).

The first author (DiBiase) appreciates the supportive conversations with her father, Reverend Anthony DiBiase, who for many years served as school counselor with antisocial youth. DiBiase is indebted to her mother, Angela DiBiase, for her enduring wisdom and support in the development of this book.

1 WELCOME TO EQUIP FOR EDUCATORS: TEACHING YOUTH (GRADES 5-8) TO THINK AND ACT RESPONSIBLY

Are you an educator (defined broadly as teacher, counselor, school administrator, or social worker)? Do you teach or counsel children, preadolescents, or young adolescents (fifth through eighth graders)? If so, we invite you to consider this curriculum for your teaching or group counseling needs. In this book, we have adapted the *treatment* program *EQUIP* (Gibbs, Potter, & Goldstein, 1995) into a broader based *prevention* curriculum. The original EQUIP program has increasingly been used by helping professionals to teach chronically antisocial or offending youths and adults to think and act responsibly. But why not intervene earlier? After all, isn't there some truth in the old adage about an ounce of prevention being worth a pound of cure? We who have adapted the original EQUIP program are Ann-Marie DiBiase (formerly at the State University of New York at Buffalo and now at Brock University, St. Catharines, Ontario), along with Beth Spring of the Northern Virginia Family Service in Oakton, Virginia, and in collaboration with authors of the original EQUIP program John Gibbs and Bud Potter (Gibbs, Goldstein, & Potter, 1995). Other contributing staff from Northern Virginia Family Service were Cyndy Dailey and Meredith McKeen. You now have in hand the product of this collaboration: *EQUIP for Educators,* a prevention curriculum.

PRIMARY AND SECONDARY PREVENTION THROUGH PSYCHOEDUCATION

Whereas EQUIP was designed for treatment (what Ellen McGinnis calls tertiary prevention in the following quotation), *EQUIP for Educators* is dedicated to the aim of prevention in either the primary or secondary sense:

> Primary Prevention is directed toward meeting the needs of the majority of the school population (80%). Students in this group do not have serious behavior problems. . . . However, given certain circumstances . . . this group may act out. The need at this level is for universal interventions, or schoolwide systems that target all students. . . . Secondary Prevention [targets] students with at-risk behaviors. This group has not responded sufficiently to primary prevention efforts and may comprise 15% of our student population. . . . Finally, Tertiary Prevention . . . is necessary for students (5%) whose patterns of behavior are more intense and chronic. (McGinnis, 2003, p. 163)

In these terms, *EQUIP for Educators* is dedicated to prevention that is either (a) primary, with the sometimes-acting-out 80 percent (requiring a universal intervention or one that targets all students at a particular grade) or (b) secondary, with the 15 percent of students who are already evidencing at-risk behaviors. In adapting EQUIP, DiBiase worked with fifth graders (primary prevention) in a Canadian health science class, while Beth Spring, Andrea Zych, and colleagues worked with selected at-risk middle and high school students (secondary prevention) in Virginia. Both primary and secondary preventive uses of *EQUIP for Educators* have therefore been field-tested.

Prevention curricula, programs, and strategies abound. The U.S. Department of Health and Human Services (Thornton, Dahlberg, Lynch, & Baer, 2000) and the U.S. Justice Department (Office of Justice Programs, 2000) provide sourcebooks containing school-, home-, and community-based strategies for preventing youth violence. Preventive character education in the elementary school is stressed at the Center for the Fourth and Fifth R's (Lickona, 2004) and other centers, programs, or projects (see Berkowitz, in press). Sharing EQUIP's heritage from the late Arnold Goldstein and colleagues' Aggression Replacement Training (Goldstein, Glick, & Gibbs, 1998) and Prepare Curriculum (Goldstein, 1999) are educational resources available from the Center on Positive Behavioral Interventions and Supports (McGinnis, 2003), the Collaborative Intensive Community Treatment Program (Amendola & Oliver, 2003), and the Center for Safe Schools and Communities (Salmon, 2003).

EQUIP for Educators shares much with these valuable psychoeducational programs and strategies. We are proud that our program is among those prevention curricula that derive at least in part from Aggression Replacement Training (ART), with its proven track record of effectiveness in schools and juvenile correctional facilities (see Goldstein et al., 1998). *Psychoeducation* refers to the teaching or training of the skills, knowledge, and mature awareness required for competent daily living (e.g., see Goldstein, 1999).

Let us say a few things about students in need of such teaching or training. First, as we note elsewhere in this book, they have more positive potential than you might think. Accordingly, you may hold them accountable for their actions and seek to inspire them with greater expectations (see Damon, 1995). To hold them accountable, after all, is to respect them, to believe in them as people with positive potential. Second, you must keep in mind that these students tend to have certain limitations or problems that can keep them from realizing their potential or rising to your greater expectations for them.

EQUIP for Educators aims to nip in the bud these problems among at-risk students. We have called these problems the "three D's": (a) developmental *delays* in moral judgment, (b) self-serving cognition *distortions,* and (c) social skill *deficiencies.* These problems are interrelated, and so are the components of *EQUIP for Educators* that address them. The components can remedy these delays, distortions, and deficiencies by equipping at-risk students with (a) mature moral judgment *(social decision making)*, (b) skills for managing anger and correcting self-serving cognitive distortions *(anger management)*, and (c) social skills for balanced and constructive social behavior *(social skills)*. It's a tough balance sometimes, but do keep faith in your students' potential for responsible thinking and acting as you address the limitations or problems that are currently obstructing their potential.

HOW DOES EQUIP FOR EDUCATORS STAND OUT?

Beyond what it shares with other programs, *EQUIP for Educators* stands out in important ways. Although the research documenting the effectiveness of ART and EQUIP (see Gibbs et al., 1995; Goldstein et al., 1998) applies, *EQUIP for Educators* has also been shown to be effective in its own right (see DiBiase, 2002). To teach and encourage students to think and act responsibly, *EQUIP for Educators* focuses on the following:

♦ Preparing a receptive interpersonal social climate (positive social culture) in the classroom

♦ Providing a rich array of opportunities for the students to take the perspectives of others

♦ Teaching students how to identify and correct their self-serving cognitive distortions, or "thinking errors"

In the following discussion, we will note the ways in which the *EQUIP for Educators* curriculum is concrete or activity oriented, as needed in working with younger students.

Equip Helps Your Students Cultivate a Positive Culture

EQUIP started in the 1990s with the recognition that psychoeducational or skills training programs for antisocial youths meet with little success unless they address the formidable challenge of the negative peer group climate. The norms (Lawrence Kohlberg called them "counternorms") of the negative peer culture disparage caring (as uncool or sissy). These norms comprise an in-your-face mentality that promotes physical aggression (e.g., "Look at me the wrong way and you're in for a fight") and other antisocial behaviors, such as stealing (e.g., "It's your fault if something is stolen—you were careless and tempting me"; Kohlberg & Higgins, 1987, p. 110). This anti-caring, "cool" (i.e., selfish and hostile) peer culture is particularly obvious at many juvenile correctional facilities, youth detention centers, and alternative schools for students with chronic antisocial or severe behavior problems. Even at a mainstream middle school, however, the negative social culture may be strong enough to undermine the behavioral impact of the prevention curriculum.

Accordingly, we have placed among the opening sessions of *EQUIP for Educators* a valuable tool for setting the right tone and climate in the classroom and promoting positive social cohesion. Called "The Martian's Adviser's Problem Situation" (fully presented in chapter 5), it is important enough to introduce here. It reads as follows:

> A man from Mars has decided to move to another planet. He has narrowed his search down to two planets, Planet A and Planet B. Planet A is a violent and dangerous place to live. People just care about themselves and don't care when they hurt others. Planet B is a safer, more peaceful place. People on Planet B do care about others. They still have fun, but they feel bad if they hurt someone. Planet B people try to make the planet a better place.
>
> **You're the Martian's adviser. Which planet should you advise him to move to?**
>
> Planet A / Planet B / can't decide *(Circle one.)*

During this opening session, students at risk for antisocial behavior can discover that they actually share values of caring underneath all their "coolness." In our experience, when students choose their planet individually and privately prior to class (preempting public pressure against caring), the majority of students choose Planet B. With assistance, the group can even become unanimous in the choice of Planet B.

You and your students can convert the classroom culture to a "Planet B" atmosphere in which psychoeducation is taken seriously. The positive potential is there. After all, every (or almost every) group member would prefer, not only for the Martian but for himself or herself, a world that is safer, more trusting, more caring. Of course, cultivating a positive culture is hard work these days, even with a younger student population. To counteract those "caring is uncool" norms, you must work to make caring fashionable (Vorrath & Brendtro, 1987). One technique is to *relabel* (Potter likes to say *right-label*) caring as strong:

> What kind of group do you want this group to be—Planet A or Planet B, negative or positive? If Planet B is what you want for this group, have you been living up to it? Planet B won't happen unless everyone works to make it happen. But it's not easy. It takes courage; it takes strength.

After the opening class session, "Planet A" and "Planet B" become part of the group vocabulary. The terms provide useful handles for contrasting student cultures: a collection of self-centered and selfish attitudes characterized by mistrust and disruption (a negative culture, Planet A) or a climate of mutual caring in word and deed, trust, and community (a positive culture, Planet B). The technique of using Planet A and Planet B as "handles" (e.g., "Did the group move toward becoming a Planet B kind of place today?") makes it easier for students who are concrete thinkers (as fifth graders and middle school students tend to be) to grasp and bring to mind clusters of attributes pertaining to negative or positive social cultures.

EQUIP HELPS YOUR STUDENTS TAKE THE PERSPECTIVES OF OTHERS

Not only can negative youth cultures be characterized as Planet A or self-centered; so can most behaviorally at-risk students! Attitudes of inflated self-esteem, entitlement, and immediate self-gratification (e.g., "Rules aren't for me"; "If I like something, it's mine"; "I want it now!") are evident in those three D's: egocentric bias in developmental moral judgment *delays* (chapter 5), self-serving cognitive *distortions* of anger (chapter 3), and imbalanced behavior that disrespects others (by threatening them, putting them down, etc.) in the *deficiencies* of social skills (chapter 4). Just as the group must convert its culture from self-centered to mutual caring, so the individual student must convert from a superficial centration upon self to a deeper, decentered stance that respects the viewpoints of others (Gibbs, 2003).

Accordingly, a fundamental theme that pervades all three components of the *EQUIP for Educators* curriculum is that of becoming less self-centered—spontaneously taking the perspectives of others. Remedying self-centered attitudes with social perspective taking is at the heart of the anger management component (chapter 3). In anger management, students are taught perspective taking and other skills to use in frustrating or provocative situations. One example is the use of positive *self-talk* such as "I can't always expect people to act the way I want them to"; "For someone to be that irritable, they must be awfully unhappy"; and "I'd be mad, too, if I were her. She has a right to expect better from me."

Social perspective taking is also at the heart of the social skills component of the *EQUIP for Educators* curriculum (chapter 4). Indeed, social skills can in many instances be construed as step-by-step, practical training to achieve balanced behavior that respects others in specific social situations. Perspective taking is implicitly involved in many of the social skills and is an explicit step in several of them. Among these are Skill 6 (Preparing for a Stressful Conversation): "How might the other person feel at the start of the stressful conversation? Why?" and Skill 9 (Dealing Constructively with Someone Accusing You of Something): "Think, 'What is the other person accusing me of? Is he or she right?'" Social skills are social perspective taking opportunities in action. In role-playing the steps of Skill 1 (Expressing a Complaint Constructively), a boy named Joe explained to the group how he had contributed to a problem: He would "run off and party" to deal with the hurt that his father would not be home to talk with him but would instead go drinking at a bar. With another student playing the role of his father, Joe considered the moment when his dad would be approachable, thought ahead to his dad's likely viewpoint, listened openly to his dad's ideas as an understanding was reached, solicited his dad's feelings about the agreement, and expressed appreciation for the his dad's cooperation. (We do not know whether Joe ever found an occasion to express his complaint constructively to his actual father, but he did become "equipped" for that and similar situations.)

Finally, in the social decision making component (chapter 5), social perspective taking opportunities are provided through discussion. Consider, for example, Angelo's Problem Situation, concerning whether Angelo should join a friend in stealing from a car. After students role-play the situation (an activity so helpful for a younger student population), they discuss the problem situation in a way that remedies egocentric bias— that is, that promotes mature morality (as well as a positive social culture). Questions such as "Let's say the car is *your* car" direct students to put themselves in the place of the prospective victim. Other questions encourage the students to take the perspectives of friends, family, and others—even those not immediately present—who would be affected by the antisocial behavior. Social perspective taking is also stimulated in the very process of the discussion, in which developmentally delayed students must justify their problem-solving decisions in the face of challenges from more developmentally advanced peers, as well as from you, the adult, as you facilitate the discussion.

EQUIP HELPS YOUR STUDENTS CORRECT THEIR THINKING ERRORS

As noted, self-centered attitudes are basic to the at-risk students who comprise negative peer cultures. In part, self-centered attitudes take the form of egocentric biases (in the context of moral judgment) and disrespectful imbalances (in the context of social skills deficiencies). It is the context of the anger management component, however, that self-centered attitudes are most aptly depicted as *distortions*. Self-centered attitudes are not just "different" or "right for them"; they are *distorted* (erroneous, inaccurate, nonveridical, faulty, wrong, etc.). In *EQUIP for Educators,* when we emphasize overcoming self-centered attitudes at the level of both the group (by promoting Planet B or a positive student culture) and individual (by promoting social perspective taking), we are doing something more directive and prescriptive than merely proposing an alternative attitude: We are correcting, or helping to correct, at-risk students' self-serving cognitive distortions or thinking *errors*.

Self-Centered is the primary self-serving cognitive distortion or thinking error. Strictly speaking, we define this error as

> according status to one's own views, expectations, needs, rights, immediate feelings, and desires to such an extent that the legitimate views, etc., of others (or even one's own long-term best interest) are scarcely considered or are disregarded altogether. (Gibbs et al., 1995, p. 108)

To the at-risk student, we say that Self-Centered

> means that you think your opinions and feelings are more important than the opinions and feelings of other people. You may not even consider how another person might feel about things. Self-Centered thinking can also mean that you think only about what you want right now and do not think about how your behaviors will affect you or others in the future. (Potter, Gibbs, & Goldstein, 2001, p. 22)

Combined with even the normal array and intensity of egocentric motives and impulses, Self-Centered is a key risk factor for aggression and other antisocial behaviors.

But Self-Centered is not the only thinking error. To continue his or her Self-Centered attitude and antisocial behavior, the at-risk student typically develops protective rationalizations, or what we view as secondary cognitive distortions. The negative peer culture's in-your-face counter-norms (as described by Kohlberg) illustrate these secondary thinking errors. Disparaging caring as "sissy" or praising behavior that harms others as "cool" illustrates *Minimizing/Mislabeling* one's destructive behavior. "Look at me the wrong way and you're in for a fight" illustrates *Assuming the Worst* about others' intentions, and "It's your fault if something is stolen—you were careless and tempting me" illustrates *Blaming Others* for one's own irresponsible behavior. Looking back on his burglaries and victims, one delinquent blamed his victims. He reflected, "If I started feeling bad, I'd say to myself, 'tough rocks for him. He should have had his house locked better and the alarm on'" (Samenow, 1984, p. 115). But at least the youth had a "bad feeling" for his victims to begin with! There's that positive potential again. When we help students to correct their thinking errors, we are helping them to refute the rationalizations that block or neutralize their empathy for actual or prospective victims. Correction of thinking errors, then, is a crucial precondition to social perspective taking.

* * *

EQUIP for Educators stands out, then, not only on emphasizing the importance of cultivating a positive student culture and on inducing social perspective taking, but also on teaching at-risk students to identify and correct their thinking errors. Although the thinking errors theme is most prominent in anger management (chapter 3), it pervades the other components of the curriculum. To teach the thinking error vocabulary, special group activities precede the curriculum sessions. As described in chapter 2, your students can play either of two games: The Millionaire Game or the EQUIPPED for Life game (Horn, Shively, & Gibbs, 2005).

The Millionaire Game, innovated by Northern Virginia Family Service and based on the popular television game show, breaks the whole student group into groups of three (a procedure used elsewhere in the program as well). These teams then compete to become "millionaires" for small prizes by correctly identifying the category of thinking error illustrated by statements such as "If I see something I like, I take it" (Self-Centered) or "If someone's careless enough to lose his wallet, he deserves to have it stolen" (Blaming Others). The EQUIPPED for Life game, available for purchase from Research Press, is highly recommended for two reasons: first, it teaches students to identify the thinking errors in *specific situational contexts* and, second, "winning" requires not only correctly naming but also *replacing* the thinking error with a more accurate thought and constructive response.

The EQUIPPED for Life game also fosters Planet B social cohesiveness. For example, a player who, after rolling the dice, lands on a space called Family Reunion must name an individual (family or friend) with whom the player would like to be reunited or a time in the past when they were reunited with someone. The Talent Show space requires the player to demonstrate a talent, and the Job Fair space requires a player to name a type of employment that interests him or her. Having the students play this game at the outset of the curriculum, then, does more than teach the thinking error vocabulary. The icing on the cake is that it also contributes to identifying and correcting problem thinking in familiar situations and encourages a positive student culture through social perspective taking.

BEYOND THIS BOOK

Your effectiveness in helping your students to think and act responsibly will be enhanced if you read beyond this book to understand the basis and larger conceptual context for EQUIP. *EQUIP for Educators* is designed to stand alone, and we do provide a brief rationale for using each of its components. Ideally, however, your use of this book should be guided by a fuller grasp of the theoretical and empirical underpinnings of the program. Accordingly, you should find study of our original program (Gibbs et al., 1995) as well as a recent broader statement (Gibbs, 2003) helpful. The original description also provides a more extensive discussion of preparatory and procedural guidelines than we can cover in this book.

Again, welcome to *EQUIP for Educators: Teaching Youth (Grades 5–8) to Think and Act Responsibly*. We hope this book will meet your prevention curriculum needs in your important work with your students. Chapters 3 through 5 describe the program components and are followed by a final session featuring an overall review exercise along with a certificate of completion that can be awarded to your students (chapter 6). But first, in the next chapter we consider the question, How do you get started? How do you prepare to teach the *EQUIP for Educators* curriculum, and how do you orient your students?

CHAPTER

2 GETTING STARTED

Having welcomed you, we need to help you get started. This chapter addresses questions of preparation and orientation: How do you prepare to teach the EQUIP curriculum? How do you orient your students to the program?

PREPARE TO TEACH

To prepare to teach the curriculum described in chapters 3 through 5, you will need to do the following:

- ◆ Decide upon course arrangements.

- ◆ Preview general procedures and teaching techniques.

- ◆ Plan how to assess your students' progress toward responsible thinking and behavior.

ORIENT STUDENTS

To orient the students, these steps are essential:

- ◆ Introduce EQUIP in a positive, motivating manner.

- ◆ Communicate the ground rules for discussions.

- ◆ Teach them to identify (and even begin to correct) the errors in their thinking.

"Getting started," then, means considering and making decisions regarding program arrangements; previewing session procedures; preparing a pretest-posttest assessment strategy; introducing EQUIP in a positive manner; explaining ground rules; and teaching the thinking errors vocabulary to be used throughout the curriculum.

COURSE ARRANGEMENTS: AN INTERRELATED AGENDA

If you look ahead to chapters 3 through 5, you will see 10 sessions each of anger management, social skills, and social decision making. Each session is designed to fit (perhaps with some adaptations) into a 45- to 50-minute class period. If your school situation permits teaching *EQUIP for Educators* three times a week, then one session for each component can be presented weekly, and the overall course will last 10 weeks. Table 2.1 depicts what such a course arrangement looks like. Of course, school situations and needs vary. You may decide to use the components as modules that you teach in sequence. That is, you would implement the 10 anger management sessions, followed by the 10 social skills sessions, and end with the 10 social decision-making sessions. In this case, we recommend beginning with the anger management component, followed by the social skills component, and then the social decision making component. You may decide to extend the course beyond 10 weeks by supplementing one or more of the components with additional materials. For example, in chapter 4 (social skills), we note the availability of additional social skills curriculum materials especially valuable for work with younger students.

Although different schedules are possible, the 10-week arrangement with interspersed sessions is optimal for teaching the *EQUIP for Educators* curriculum. Regarding the overall time frame, a period of less than several months may not be sufficient for the curriculum concepts to jell and truly influence students toward responsible thinking and acting. Regarding the agenda, teaching across all three components each week brings out the interrelationships among them. For example, "thinking ahead" makes its appearance as self-talk in anger management (chapter 3), as a step in constructive social behavior in social skills (chapter 4), and as consideration for others in mature social decision making (chapter 5). Each manifestation of the concept facilitates its mastery in other curriculum contexts. In another example, role-playing the social skill Dealing Constructively with Negative Peer Pressure (Skill 3) can be expected to facilitate mature reasoning and decisions in social decision making, in which many of the problem situations entail negative peer pressure. And, working in the other direction, the mature judgment and decisions achieved in social decision making can be expected to enlighten students' use of social skills such as Helping Others (Skill 5). After all, the best way to help a friend must be considered carefully when the requested "help" would mean joining in theft from a car (Angelo's Problem Situation), letting a friend steal or cheat (Sabrina's and Angelo's Problem Situations, respectively), or keeping quiet about a friend's or relative's drug trafficking, escape, or school shooting plans (Greg's, Lamar's, and Joe's Problem Situations, respectively).

Furthermore, it is optimal to teach an anger management session first, followed by social skills and social decision making. In our experience, many at-risk students readily acknowledge that they have a

Table 2.1 The 10-Week EQUIP for Educators Curriculum: Agenda and Main Features

Anger Management/ Thinking Error Correction	Social Skills	Social Decision Making
1 **Evaluating anger/aggression** Reevaluating, relabeling Anger management, not elimination	2 **Expressing a Complaint Constructively** Think ahead what you'll say Say how you contributed to problem Make a constructive suggestion	3 **Martian's Adviser's Problem Situation** *Key value: Affiliation* Planet A seen as self-centered Planet B labeled truly strong Guiding students toward Planet B
4 **Anatomy of anger (AMBC)** Self-talk (mind) as a source of anger Early warning signs (body) Anger-reducing self-talk	5 **Caring for Someone Who Is Sad or Upset** Notice and think ahead Listen, don't interrupt	6 **Jerry's and Mateo's Problem Situations** *Key values: Relationships and respect* Value of close friendships Breaking up in a considerate way Getting even is immature
7 **Monitoring/correcting thinking errors** John's Thinking Errors exercise Daily logs	8 **Dealing Constructively with Negative Peer Pressure** Think, "Why?" Think ahead to consequences Suggest something else (less harmful)	9 **Jeff's Problem Situation** *Key values: Honesty and respect for property* Can't trust friend with a stealing problem Stealing is wrong even if from a stranger
10 **Relaxation Techniques for Reducing Anger** Deep breathing, backward counting, peaceful imagery Anger reducers to buy time	11 **Keeping Out of Fights** Stop and think Think ahead to consequences Handle the situation another way.	12 **Angelo's and Sabrina's Problem Situations** *Key values: Honesty and respect for property* Shouldn't let friend steal Harm from stealing True friend wouldn't put you on the spot Closing the gap between judgment and behavior (relabeling, using social skills)

Note: Numbers at the top of boxes indicate the order in which the different types of meetings are held.

Table 2.1 (continued)

Anger Management/ Thinking Error Correction	Social Skills	Social Decision Making

13
Thinking Ahead to Consequences
  Thinking ahead (if-then thinking)
	14
	Helping Others
	  Think, "Is there a need?"
	  Think ahead how to help, when to offer to help
		15
		Greg's and Lamar's Problem Situations
		  Key values: Quality of life, life
		  Should tell on drug-dealing brother
		  Others could get killed
		  Important to send drug dealers to jail

16
Using "I" Statements for Achieving Constructive Consequences
  "You" statements (put-downs, threats)
  Use of "I" statements instead of "you" statements
	17
	Preparing for a Stressful Conversation
	  Imagine ahead your feelings, the other person's feelings
	  Think ahead what to say
	  Think ahead how the other person might reply
		18
		Duane's Problem Situation
		  Key value: Quality of life
		  Shouldn't deliver drugs for friend
		  Sister's life may be at stake
		  Closing gap between judgment and behavior (relabeling, correcting thinking errors, exhorting)

19
Self-Evaluation
  Self-evaluation, self-reflection
  Talking back to thinking errors
  Staying constructive
	20
	Dealing Constructively with Someone Angry at You
	  Listen openly and patiently
	  Think of something you can agree with, say the person is right about that
	  Apologize or explain, make a constructive suggestion
		21
		Joe's Problem Situation
		  Key value: Life
		  Should tell on suicidal friend
		  Suicide is Self-Centered error
		  Existential/spiritual concerns

22
Reversing
  Things you do that make other people angry
  Reversing exercise (correcting Blaming Others error)
	23
	Expressing Care and Appreciation
	  Think if the person would like to know you care
	  Think ahead what you'll say, when
	  Tell the person how you feel
		24
		Shane's Problem Situation
		  Key values: Honesty and respect for property
		  Should tell on friend who shoplifted
		  Important to prosecute shoplifters
		  Store owner is not to blame

Anger Management/ Thinking Error Correction	Social Skills	Social Decision Making
25 **Victims and Victimizers** Think of the other person (TOP) Consequences for victims	26 **Dealing Constructively with Someone Accusing You of Something** Think how you feel, tell yourself to calm down Think if the accuser is right If the accuser is right, apologize/make restitution; if wrong, say it is not true, it is a wrong impression	27 **Alfonso's Problem Situation** *Key value: Honesty* Shouldn't help friend cheat Can't trust "friend" with cheating problem
28 **Grand Review** Learning how to say why you are angry without put-downs and what you want the other person to do	29 **Responding Constructively to Failure** Ask yourself if you did fail Think what you could do differently Decide on a plan to try again	30 **Regina's Problem Situation** *Key values: Quality of life and truth* Should reveal violent dad's drinking Should do what's best for family Wouldn't want someone to lie to you But mother wrong to put Regina on spot

31
The Final Session: Up or Down?

Up represents mature, accurate, constructive, responsible.

Down represents immature, inaccurate, distorted, destructive, irresponsible.

Spans all three curriculum components and provides opportunities for motivational comments.

Tests knowledge of the content of curriculum components.

Encourages the use of concepts or skills learned in sessions to help others and self.

problem with controlling their temper, so the need to learn how to manage anger is obvious to them. They can build from skills for staying calm (anger management); to learning, through the concrete activity of role-playing, how to act constructively (social skills); to ways to make mature decisions (social decision making) in difficult social problem situations. Also, the social skills role plays tend to "warm up" the group to the problem situation discussions (as do the role plays of the problems themselves).

SESSION PROCEDURES AND TECHNIQUES

Acquaint yourself with the *EQUIP for Educators* curriculum, session by session (as described in chapters 3 through 5). Note any preparations or materials that may be required for the sessions. An easel pad is necessary for many of the sessions. Before each session, check the availability of paper for the pad, two markers (preferably different colors, to distinguish ideas), and masking tape to hang the completed sheets on the wall. If possible, plan to leave the sheets posted; they will be a useful reference and reminder in subsequent sessions. Also, photocopy sufficient numbers of any student handout materials that may be pertinent.

You will note some format and procedural features that are common across the curriculum. After the first week, the sessions typically begin with a brief review of the previous session and end with a comment that introduces the topic of the next session. Each session description provides an overview of student expectations and activities and educator notes—these are well worth studying.

The key features of your role as session facilitator are highlighted in the Educator's Review and Self-Evaluation Form provided for each curriculum component (see Figures 3.10, 4.5, and 5.5 in the chapters devoted to these components). Following any of the sessions are certain general concerns: Did the students follow the ground rules? Were they interested and involved? Did you find constructive value in every serious student comment, and speak in a respectful rather than threatening or demanding tone?

USING WORKING TRIADS

Subgroups of three (i.e., triads) are used for many instructional purposes. Typically, at an appropriate point during the session, students form working triads for the given activity and, upon its completion, reconvene in the larger group. Before beginning the sessions, you will need to prepare a strategy for breaking down your group of 20 or 30 students into triads. Your strategy for forming triads will be needed immediately: A pre-course activity, The Millionaire Game, is played by teams of three each.

Part of your plan may be to suggest that the partners in the groups of three get to know one another by asking each student to name a pet, if the student has one, or a favorite type of music, movie, or place. Reserve some time at the outset for the triad partners to get comfortable with one another.

There are many ways to form working triads. One useful approach involves using a deck of cards to determine group composition and the parts students take on during the triad activity. The procedure for a class of 27 students is as follows:

1. In advance, select three suits (e.g., hearts, clubs, diamonds).

2. From the cards of these suits, select 2s through 10s (a total of three cards per suit, or 27 cards).

3. Shuffle and hand out the cards, one card per student.

4. Have students find others who have a matching number (e.g., all the 2s must find each other) and form a triad.

5. At this point, you may tell students that the suit of the card determines the role the student will play in the triad. For example:

   Students holding a heart become *speakers* (presenting results to the class).

   Students holding a diamond become *recorders* (recording answers or taking notes on the activity).

   Students holding a club become the *equipment people* (retrieving paper, art supplies, or any other materials needed for the activity).

   Students find this procedure for forming triads equitable; and, when given a chance to form their own groups, they often express a desire to use the cards in this way.

> Use this procedure every second time you ask students to form triads. Forming new triads conveys the idea that the students are a team and that they must learn to work with as many peers as possible. Leaving the students in the same triad for more than two activities may invite opportunities for conflict.

FACILITATING ROLE PLAY

In your preview of session procedures and teaching techniques, you will notice places where you are to facilitate role play, which is conducted in the working triads. Because it is a prevention curriculum designed for younger students, *EQUIP for Educators* particularly emphasizes role-play activity, not only in the teaching of social skills but also in social decision making and in some anger management sessions. To facilitate student role plays, you should follow these guidelines:

◆ Wait until the students in the group or class are acquainted and at ease with one another.

- Make sure both observers and players fully understand the role-play situation and its context or relevance before it is enacted.

- Anticipate some self-consciousness on the part of the students. You can help them feel at ease by making clear that their role-playing is not a theatrical performance—they will not be judged on how well they can act.

- Without coercing anyone, try to induce as many students to participate as possible. Particularly shy students can ease into role-playing by first playing supporting or "coactor" roles for other students (Goldstein, 1993).

- Make clear that observers should be attentive but quiet and unobtrusive during the role play.

- Quickly facilitate the conclusion of a role play if a student is beginning to engage in inappropriate personal disclosures.

USING THE "SANDWICH STYLE" OF CONSTRUCTIVE CRITICISM

These checklists also ask whether in the session you maintained a balance between criticism and approval by using the *sandwich style of constructive criticism* (in which a critical comment is preceded and followed by supportive ones). An example of a sandwich-style comment would be "The group has been moving so well toward Planet B [support] that I know today's Planet A behavior [criticism] was just a temporary setback. Such a strong group will be able to overcome that setback [support]." The sandwich-style comment does represent a balance. On the one hand, simple rewards or approval must be given sparingly as a precaution against the tendency of at-risk students to overgeneralize any positive comments as a blanket approval of their antisocial behavior (Yochelson & Samenow, 1976). By the same token, simple criticism can also be overgeneralized—as a blanket rejection. Where the criticism is balanced with just one positive comment, the balanced style has been called *punch and burp* (e.g., "That was childish behavior [criticism] and not like you. You are much more mature than that [compliment]; Vorrath & Brendtro, 1985, p. 111) or (in the other sequence) *pat and swat* (e.g., "You are too valuable [pat] to continue doing stupid things to yourself [swat] . . . hurting others hurts oneself;" Agee, 1979, p. 37).

USING THE "ASK, DON'T TELL" TECHNIQUE

Another key technique indicated in the checklists is called *ask, don't tell*. The questioning style is characterized by Tom Lickona (1983) as the "ask-don't-tell method of reasoning with kids" (p. 302). By nature, questions stimulate the listener to think. Harry Vorrath and Larry Brendtro (1985) depict the value of this method:

> While several group members all talk simultaneously, a highly perceptive comment from one youth goes unnoticed. The [educator] does not tell the group, "You shouldn't all be talking at once," or make any other directive comment. Rather, he only needs to ask, "Did the group hear Ronald's question?" (p. 73)

As with any technique, the ask, don't tell method must be applied properly. Lickona (1983) suggests that proper questions are those that stimulate children to consider positive, constructive, prosocial alternatives. For instance, the educator might ask a dawdling group, "What do group members need to do to make this a helpful session today?" Improper questions are those that attempt to shame ("Can't the group act better than a bunch of 2-year-olds today?"), embarrass ("What kind of impression would that give anyone visiting this group?"), or intimidate ("Do you know what I'm going to do if I catch any of you doing that?"). Such questions direct group attention toward pleasing others or avoiding detection and punishment rather than toward recognizing that certain actions are harmful or unfair to others. Where a student seems to be evidencing a thinking error, ask, don't tell (e.g., "Ron, are you assuming the worst about your future?") is especially appropriate; after all, few of us can read minds. Where punishment must be enforced, the appeal should not be personally threatening but should instead be objective and information oriented (e.g., "Does the group remember what the consequence is when a group member's practice work isn't done?").

The style and tone of the questions are also important. Your questions should be simple and brief, asked one at a time (asking several questions at once can be confusing). Again, as indicated on the checklist, the questioner should maintain a normal voice volume and speak in a respectful rather than a threatening or demanding tone. In this connection, Lickona (1983) notes an added dividend of the ask, don't tell method: If the educator has become angry or distressed at a turn of events in the meeting, asking a question (even an "I" question—e.g., "Why am I upset right now?") lets him or her regain emotional control as the responsibility for talking shifts immediately to the group. Furthermore, the question doesn't put the group on the defensive as a statement might, and it gives the group a chance to recognize and correct the unfairness or harmfulness of their actions.

The ask, don't tell method can be overused. Lickona's advice is to "ask questions when it feels natural to do so, and make a direct statement when it feels natural to do that" (1983, p. 322). Indeed, avoiding direct statements altogether would virtually preclude the teaching that needs to take place. Those using *EQUIP for Educators* in a primary prevention context, with students in the fifth grade, may especially need to use direct statements. Used to an appropriate degree, the ask, don't tell method is an excellent tool for stimulating your students to stay focused on the psychoeducational tasks of thinking and acting responsibly.

By the way, as part of getting started, you may wish to sit down and use the ask, don't tell technique with yourself! You could ask yourself important preparatory questions, such as "Have I gotten the principal on board so students will take EQUIP seriously?"; "Will the students know that the school disciplinary policies still apply?"; and "How am I going to break the class down into triads without opening the door to chaos?" If you do so, you will be stimulating *yourself* to do some much-needed preparatory thinking and planning.

PRETEST AND POSTTEST ASSESSMENT

If at all possible, you should include in your planning some strategy for assessing the effectiveness of the curriculum. Cost-benefit analyses of school programs, increasingly mandated these days, are of course difficult to accomplish in the absence of any systematic outcome information. Relative to some suitable comparison group, does your *EQUIP for Educators* group show significant declines in, say, referrals to the principal's office, suspensions, or truancy? Do students involved in the program show significant improvements in teacher ratings of classroom conduct? In academic grades or graduation rates?

In addition to the assessment of overt behavioral outcomes, you should try to assess (if possible) whether the curriculum is helping the students to develop the skills and maturity representing the goals of the intervention. So part of assessment planning is selecting appropriate psychological assessment instruments. Preferably, your measures could be administered both before and after the curriculum period. We generally recommend the use of psychometrically developed assessment instruments, especially for the three areas specifically corresponding to the EQUIP curriculum: anger management, social skills, and social decision making (mature moral judgment). Measures we have developed or found to be most helpful in these areas include the following.

How I Think (HIT) Questionnaire: Developed by Gibbs, Barriga, and Potter (2001), the How I Think (HIT) Questionnaire is available, along with the *How I Think (HIT) Questionnaire Manual* (Barriga, Gibbs, Potter, & Liau, 2001), from Research Press. The HIT targets the more seriously at-risk student.

Children's Inventory of Anger: For milder or younger populations (children and adolescents in grades 1–11), the Children's Inventory of Anger (Nelson & Finch, 2000; completion time 10–15 minutes) may be more appropriate.

Inventory of Adolescent Problems–Short Form (IAP–SF): Developed by Gibbs, Swillinger, Leeman, Simonian, Rowland, and Jaycox (1995) the Inventory of Adolescent Problems–Short Form (IAP–SF) for assessing social skills is given as Appendix B in the original EQUIP program guide (Gibbs et al., 1995). The IAP–SF targets adolescents or preadolescents grades 6 and higher. It must be administered as an individual interview.

Social Skills Rating Scale (SSRS): A measure that may be administered with groups of children from kindergarten through secondary school (K–12) is the Social Skills Rating Scale (SSRS; Gresham & Elliot, 1990; completion time approximately 25 minutes).

Sociomoral Reflection Measure-Short Form (SRM–SF): The SRM-SF (completion time: approximately 20 minutes, for group administration with individuals 12 years to adult), administration guidelines, scoring manual, rating form, and self-training materials are provided in *Moral Maturity: Measuring the Development of Sociomoral Reflection* (Gibbs, Basinger, & Fuller, 1992). The SRM-SF can be administered to younger children in an individualized context.

PREPARING THE STUDENTS

INTRODUCING THE CURRICULUM

Any introductory remarks made to the students before the course begins should be positive and motivating, and should communicate that the course work will be "serious business." The comments should convey faith in the students' potential to help one another and themselves achieve more positive behavior. If at all possible, your school principal should make the bulk of the comments to drive home how seriously the program is taken at the highest levels. Demonstrating that the curriculum has the support of the principal may be especially important if the curriculum is to be used with more seriously at-risk students selected for a secondary prevention program.

The principal might liken the prospective EQUIP group to an athletic team, making the following points:

◆ You are all going to get a chance to start and develop a good team, a *winning* team, whose team members succeed in life.

◆ Like a coach helping a team, your teacher (or counselor) will help you become strong enough to help one another and yourselves to develop positive thinking and behavior.

◆ To coach your development, your teacher (or counselor) will give you certain equipment (that's why the course is called EQUIP) or help you develop certain skills. These skills will help you to think straight, manage your anger, deal constructively with others, and make more mature decisions in difficult situations.

◆ When you don't think straight, you make mistakes in your thinking that disrespect others. If you think it's okay to take something that belongs to someone else just because you want it, that's called a "thinking error," and you can't be part of a winning team if you don't learn to correct it. Before you can correct thinking errors, you have to learn to identify them. So before the course begins, you will participate in some group activities to learn this important vocabulary.

◆ Also before the course begins, you will be coached on how to help one another—in particular, how to talk with one another in a positive way. In a special session, we will "discuss how to discuss"—that is, will teach certain ground rules for talking with one another.

◆ Your coach can prepare and guide you but cannot play the game for you. It will be up to you to help your teammates—and at the same time help yourself—to get good enough to win. You do have the power, the potential to make it happen.

COMMUNICATING GROUND RULES

If possible, you should devote a special advance class to the ground rules that will govern activity-related discussions during the EQUIP sessions. For this discussion and the ones to follow, the students should, if possible, be sitting in a circle so they can see each other as they interact. To structure the discussion and help the students remember the rules, you may distribute a list like the one shown in Table 2.2. Use the bracketed questions to prompt constructive discussion of the rationale for

Table 2.2   Ground Rules for EQUIP Discussions

1. *Attend to the speaker.*

   [How would you feel if someone was playing with something or writing while you were sharing your thoughts, feelings, and behaviors?]

2. *Each student must be involved and participate.*

   [Why is it important for the group that everyone be involved?]

3. *Only one student talks at a time.*

   [If by mistake you interrupt someone, what should you say to him or her?]

4. *Listen to the other person who is talking.*

   [Is waiting your turn to talk the same as listening?]

5. *If you disagree with someone, do so respectfully.*

   [Why is this important?]

6. *If you criticize a fellow student, give him or her a chance to respond.*

   [How do you feel when you are criticized? Why is it important to give the person a chance to respond?]

7. *Never put down or threaten anyone.*

   [How are put-downs and threats negative? What would be positive things to say instead?]

8. *Stay focused on the subject.*

   [Why is it important for participants to stay on the subject?]

9. *Remember who said what.*

   [Why is it important for participants to remember?]

10. *Everything personal that is shared in the room, stays in the room.*

    [What does "confidentiality" mean? Why is it important for every participant to respect confidentiality?]

each rule. It is helpful to print the rules on a large sheet of chart paper and post them in the room where EQUIP instruction takes place. (The ground rules listed in Table 2.2 are given in the Appendix without the bracketed questions.)

TEACHING THINKING ERRORS

Important not only for anger management but also for social skills and social decision making is learning the self-serving cognitive distortions called *thinking errors* ("faulty beliefs," "stinking thinking," etc.). The thinking error vocabulary is so important to EQUIP that we recommend you devote another advance class to teach it.

The easiest way to teach the thinking errors is through a game format. Either of the two games can be used. Beth Spring, Andrea Zych, and others at Northern Virginia Family Service have developed The Millionaire Game, adapted from a popular television game show. The Millionaire Game will introduce the thinking error vocabulary. Going beyond the Millionaire game is the EQUIPPED for Life game (Horn et al., 2005), available for purchase from Research Press. (If you decide to use the EQUIPPED for Life game, be sure to specify the version for grades 5–8.)

Both games start by introducing students to the four thinking errors. Display the four errors in a whole-class format (on an easel pad, chalkboard, overhead projector) in the form of a grid, as shown in Figure 2.1. Separately, provide the thinking errors definitions (see Figure 2.2). It is helpful to post the thinking errors definitions prominently in the room where EQUIP instruction will take place. (The EQUIPPED for Life game provides the definitions on a game card.)

The Millionaire Game

The Millionaire Game breaks the group down into teams of three (the first use of the triad procedure) to see who can correctly name the greatest number of thinking error statements. The items on the Thinking Errors Questions: Answer Key (Table 2.3) are drawn from the How I Think Questionnaire, discussed earlier in this chapter. (If you are using the full HIT as an assessment instrument, you will need to decide whether it is acceptable to "teach to the test" to some extent.) In this game, each participant wins a million dollars, represented by a small prize (e.g., a 100 Grand candy bar or another type of candy bar). Guidelines for conducting the game are as follows:

1. Photocopy and cut apart the Thinking Errors Statements Cards from the Appendix, or copy the statements on separate index cards. Mix the cards up thoroughly.

2. Display the four thinking errors names in a grid and the definitions of the errors. Explain that the group, in teams, can win prizes if they can correctly name the thinking errors illustrated in certain questions.

3. Present yourself as the game show host, who will be asking the questions.

4. Break down the group into three-person teams (triads).

5. Apportion the cards into batches of five. You will need the same number of batches of five as you have teams.

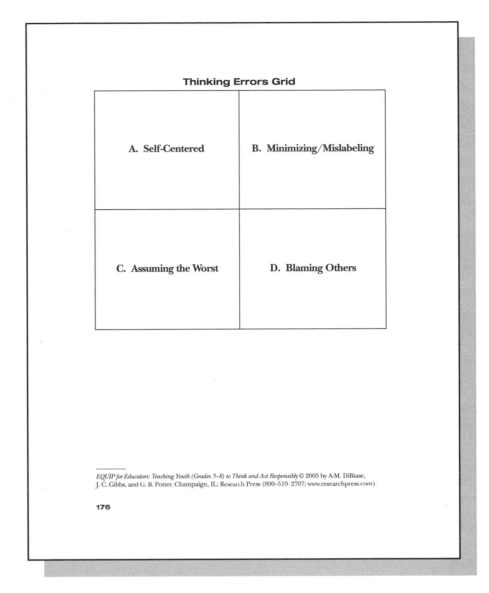

Thinking Errors Grid

A. Self-Centered	B. Minimizing/Mislabeling
C. Assuming the Worst	D. Blaming Others

EQUIP for Educators: Teaching Youth (Grades 5–8) to Think and Act Responsibly © 2005 by A-M. DiBiase, J. C. Gibbs, and G. B. Potter. Champaign, IL: Research Press (800–519–2707; www.researchpress.com).

176

Figure 2.1   Thinking Errors Grid

Thinking Errors Definitions

A. Self-Centered	Self-Centered thinking means that you think your opinions and feelings are more important than the opinions and feelings of other people. You may not even consider how another person might feel about things. Self-Centered thinking can also mean that you think only about what you want right now and do not think about how your behaviors will affect you or others in the future.
B. Minimizing/Mislabeling	Minimizing/Mislabeling means that you think your problems or behaviors are not as wrong or harmful as they really are. You put a label on your bad behavior to make it sound okay or good, or you describe someone with a bad name (like *snitch* or *fool*) so it will seem okay to hurt the person.
C. Assuming the Worst	Assuming the Worst means that you think everyone is out to get you (or someone else). *(Example:* If someone accidentally bumps into you in the hall, you assume the person did it on purpose instead of thinking it was an accident.) Assuming the Worst about yourself means that you think only bad things can happen to you and that you can't do anything about it. Assuming the Worst can also mean that you think you or other people will not be able to change or make improvements or do anything about bad things that happen in life.
D. Blaming Others	Blaming Others means that you do not take responsibility for your own behavior, but instead blame other people for harmful behavior when it is really your fault. You may think you can harm innocent others—that they deserve it because people in the past treated you badly. Blaming Others can also mean that you think your bad behaviors are okay because you were on drugs or alcohol or in a bad mood.

EQUIP for Educators: Teaching Youth (Grades 5–8) to Think and Act Responsibly © 2005 by A-M. DiBiase, J. C. Gibbs, and G. B. Potter. Champaign, IL: Research Press (800–519–2707; www.researchpress.com).

177

Figure 2.2   Thinking Errors Definitions

Chapter 2

Table 2.3   Thinking Errors Questions: Answer Key

Self-Centered

1. Sometimes you have to lie to get what you want.

2. If I see something I like, I take it.

3. When I get mad, I don't care who gets hurt.

4. If I really want something, it doesn't matter how I get it.

5. You should get what you need, even if it means someone has to get hurt.

6. Rules are mostly meant for other people.

7. Getting what you need is the only important thing.

8. If I lied to someone, that's my business.

Blaming Others

9. If I made a mistake, it's because I got mixed up with the wrong crowd.

10. If someone leaves a car unlocked, they are asking to have it stolen.

11. It's OK to tell a lie if someone is dumb enough to fall for it.

12. People force you to lie if they ask too many questions.

13. People are always trying to start fights with me.

14. If someone is careless enough to lose a wallet, they deserve to have it stolen.

15. If people don't cooperate with me, it's not my fault if someone gets hurt.

16. When I lose my temper, it's the fault of people who make me mad.

Minimizing/Mislabeling

17. People need to be roughed up once in a while.

18. You have to get even with people who don't show you respect.

19. Everybody lies—it's no big deal.

20. If you know you can get away with it, only a fool wouldn't steal.

Table 2.3 Thinking Errors Questions: Answer Key (continued)

21. Only a coward would ever walk away from a fight.

22. Stores make enough money that it's OK to just take things you need.

23. A lie doesn't really matter if you don't know that person.

24. Everybody breaks the law—it's no big deal.

Assuming the Worst

25. I can't help losing my temper a lot.

26. You can't trust people because they will always lie to you.

27. It's no use trying to stay out of fights.

28. No matter how hard I try, I can't help getting in trouble.

29. If you don't push people around, you will always get picked on.

30. You might as well steal. If *you* don't take it, somebody else will.

31. I might as well lie—when I tell the truth, people don't believe me anyway.

32. Everybody steals—you might as well get your share.

6. Choose one team and read aloud one batch of statements, allowing them to respond to each item. If the team is sure of the right answer after conferring, they can announce their choice. If the team is not sure, they can use a "lifeline," including "take away two" or "ask the audience." For "take away two," the game show host (you) covers up two of the four thinking errors, leaving the students with a choice between just two possibilities. Or the teams can "ask the audience." (The audience consists of the other teams, who are listening while they are waiting their turn.)

7. Give each team as much time as is feasible to arrive at a final answer. If the team offers a final answer different from the answer according to the key, they can argue for their reward by explaining how they see the statement as an example of the thinking error they picked. The thinking errors are so intimately interrelated that several statements can be seen as illustrating more than one error. Clearly incorrect answers do not qualify the team for a prize.

8. Award the prizes after each team completes its answers.

9. Continue until all teams are done.

The EQUIPPED for Life Game

Just as *EQUIP for Educators* is adapted for prevention purposes with students in grades 5–8, so now is our therapeutic board game, *EQUIPPED for Life*. We can offer this game thanks to the pioneering work of Mary Horn, EQUIP Services Coordinator at Alvis House, an organization of community-based facilities in central Ohio. As noted, the new edition of the game (Horn, Shively, & Gibbs, 2005) offers a version appropriate for students in this age range. If it is at all feasible, we recommend that you purchase a sufficient number of game boxes for your class. As many as four participants can play each game. For a class of 20, then, you would need a minimum of five game boards; if you wish to break the class down into triads, you would need more.

The EQUIPPED for Life game goes beyond The Millionaire Game as a teaching tool in several ways. Although the statements used in The Millionaire Game are drawn from the actual thinking of offenders, they do not arise from a specific context, and "winning" merely means correctly naming the type of error. The statements used in the EQUIPPED for Life game are presented as the thoughts and behaviors of an individual in one or another familiar social situation. Furthermore, to "win," a player must not only correctly identify the thinking error but must also suggest as a replacement an accurate thought and constructive response. In this way, this game goes beyond teaching the concepts and begins to teach responsible thinking and acting.

Central to the game are situation cards. The majority of the situation cards narrate a particular situation or vignette in a particular area (School/Community, Employment/After-School Activities, Relationships, or Substance Abuse). A player selects a situation card at random from a pile on the board if his or her game piece lands on a situation card space. For example, a player might pick a card that reads, "An older friend asks you to be a lookout while she steals a pair of shoes. You think, 'I'm just a lookout—it's not like I'm the one stealing the shoes.'" To collect an EQUIP chip, the player must do two things. First, the player must correctly identify the thinking error in the response (in the example, it is Minimizing/Mislabeling because the individual is trying the minimize active participation in a theft by characterizing his or her role as being "just a lookout"). Second, the player must replace the erroneous thinking with an accurate thought (perhaps "I'd be helping her steal") and suggest a constructive response (perhaps "I'll say no and suggest we go to a movie"). The player who acquires the greatest number of chips wins the game.

INTRODUCING THE MARTIAN'S ADVISER'S PROBLEM SITUATION

As shown in Table 2.1, the Martian's Adviser's Problem Situation is presented in Session 3 in the curriculum, the first in the social decision making curriculum component. However, at your discretion, you may use this situation to begin the curriculum. As such, the situation becomes an *advance organizer,* to set the stage for the information and activities to follow.

> We hope in this chapter that we have provided enough guidance to help you get started. You and your students may now be sufficiently prepared and oriented to embark upon the *EQUIP for Educators* curriculum as described in the next three chapters.

CHAPTER 3
EQUIPPING WITH SKILLS TO MANAGE ANGER AND CORRECT THINKING ERRORS

> [Mike] barged madly up the steps into the house [Pioneer House, a residential treatment center for "out-of-control" preadolescent boys]. Luckily, this time the door was open so the usual pounding, kicking of door, etc., wasn't necessary. I was in my [Director's] office tied up in a phone call and the door was closed. Mike yelled for me, shouting something about his jack knife which I was keeping in the drawer for him. I put my hand over the receiver and said, "O.K., come in." But the lock had slipped on the door and he couldn't open it. Before I even had a chance to excuse myself from my phone conversation and say, "Just a minute, I'll be back" he was pounding on the door, kicking it, calling me a "sonofabitch" repetitively. I opened the door and gave him his knife. Even this failed to quiet his furor, and when I commented on the obvious fact that I hadn't even meant to make him wait, that the lock had slipped, all I got was a snarling, contemptuous "shit." (Redl & Wineman, 1951, p. 92)

Although "thoughtless" or impulsive to an extent, anger and aggression also involve self-serving cognitive distortions. Cognitive distortions are inaccurate ways of perceiving events. They have also been called *errors of thinking* (Yochelson & Samenow, 1976, 1977, 1986) or *faulty beliefs* (Ellis, 1977). In the preceding quotation, Mike's self-centered sense of entitlement ("How dare he make me wait!") was a cognitive distortion that figured powerfully in his anger and aggression. Aaron Beck (1999, p. 25) was correct to characterize self-centered entitlement as the center or "eye ('I') of the storm" of violent behavior—indeed, it is the self-centered ego or "I" (Freud's word was *id*) that generates the storm!

Much of the anger management training in the *EQUIP for Educators* program emphasizes the correction of Self-Centered and other thinking errors, in addition to teaching the use of techniques like slow, deep breathing and imaging peaceful scenes. Correcting thinking errors is so important for responsible thinking and acting that we had you teach the thinking error vocabulary even before the start of the curriculum (see chapter 2).

SCOPE OF THE ANGER MANAGEMENT COMPONENT

In the following pages, we outline the 10-week instructional format. Each session after the first one begins with a review of the previous session and usually concludes with a reference to the topic of the next session. As with the other components, many of the sessions will require a marker and easel pad. As a sheet is filled, you may ask a student to remove it and tape it to the classroom wall for future reference.

The anger management curriculum component becomes more direct and specific as the sessions progress. The early sessions provide students with the opportunity to step back and learn about anger and aggression "from a distance." The students learn, for example, the key role of the mind in creating the storm of anger and violence. With each passing week, however, as the students become more objective and less defensive, the teaching applies more specifically to their own aggressive behavior and its consequences. (In Session 7, for example, students list two things they do to aggravate others.) The final session offers a grand review that summarizes the teaching of this component. Table 3.1 provides a week-by-week description of the anger management component of the *EQUIP for Educators* curriculum.

Table 3.1   The 10-Week Format for Equipping with Skills to Manage Anger and Correct Thinking Errors

Week 1	Evaluating and Relabeling Anger/Aggression
Week 2	Key Role of Mind in Anger
	Monitoring Mind and Body
	Reducing Anger
Week 3	Monitoring and Correcting Thinking Errors
Week 4	Relaxation Techniques for Reducing Anger: Relaxation
Week 5	Powerful Self-Talk Techniques for Reducing Anger: Thinking Ahead to Consequences and TOP (Think of the Other Person)
Week 6	Achieving Constructive Consequences
Week 7	Self-Evaluation
Week 8	Reversing
Week 9	Victims and Victimizers
Week 10	Grand Review

After each anger management session, you should review your role as an educator in the session. Evaluate your effectiveness in terms of the four phases of each session by filling out a copy of the Educator's Review and Self-Evaluation Form (Anger Management/Thinking Error Correction) for each triad. A reproducible copy of this form is given as Figure 3.10, at the end of the chapter.

Evaluating and Relabeling Anger/Aggression

OVERVIEW OF EXPECTATIONS AND ACTIVITIES

Students will . . .

◆ Discuss anger, aggression, and the benefits of controlling anger.

◆ Identify the thinking errors in their attitudes toward aggression and violence. Especially, students will *relabel* (or *"right-label"*) anger/aggression (as self-centered, immature, counterproductive) and nonviolence (as putting children in a stronger position by giving them options besides fighting).

PROCEDURE AND EDUCATOR NOTES

Begin with a discussion of anger and aggression that invites students to step back from anger and see its advantages and disadvantages. Say something like:

> If you get angry pretty often, it must have some advantages for you. You also may have noticed some disadvantages of letting your anger get out of control.

During the discussion, point out that anger can be good if it is controlled or managed to motivate constructive behavior. Point out that the goal is to manage or control—not to eliminate—your anger. Aggression may sometimes be justified for legitimate self-defense. Start the relabeling:

> Strong people (boys/girls who are truly cool) control their anger. Successful athletes are powerful because they use self-control. *(Provide examples.)* Self-Control makes you a winner, not a wimp.

> If aggression is your only option, you are the weak or dependent one.

As the children discuss the advantages and disadvantages of anger/aggression, list these advantages and disadvantages (or benefits of controlling anger) in separate columns on an easel pad. When the list is completed, you may post it in your room for future reference. Some themes that might arise in the discussion include the following:

Self-defense: "To protect myself"; "So no one will step on me"; "So others will not take advantage of me"

Power: "Makes me feel big, powerful, superior"; "Then I'm free to get things, do what I want"

Vengeance: "To get even"; "To not let others get away with putting me down or pushing me around"

Look for chances to ask about the thinking errors and sociomoral immaturity in these advantages:

Self-defense: "I was only defending or protecting myself" can often be an excuse (Minimizing/Mislabeling) for unprovoked aggression.

Power: To hurt others so that you can "do what you want" fails to respect others (Self-Centered).

Vengeance: Hurting others to get even reflects a low-level eye-for-an-eye, tooth-for-a-tooth morality.

The longer the students talk about the supposed advantages—especially if you highlight the immaturity or thinking errors and right-label the out-of-control aggression—the more they may start to mention some disadvantages:

Instead of self-defense: Instead of preventing others from "stepping on you," often aggression only "causes more problems, more fights, makes things worse."

Instead of power: Instead of feeling big or powerful, you may feel "stupid," "embarrassed," or "sorry." (Probe "sorry" to see if it entails feeling bad for harming others.) Countering a "rush" or feelings of power from pushing people around are the points that "you lose friends" because they "can't trust you" and that other people fear you but "don't respect you, don't want to be around you."

After vengeance: After you get even, "the other person would get angry, could try to get back at you."

Display the Clown—or Clowns?—in the Ring diagram (Figure 3.1) in a whole-class format to drive home the relabeling of anger/aggression as weak or foolish. Explain the following:

The clown in the circus ring is someone who is trying to start a fight.

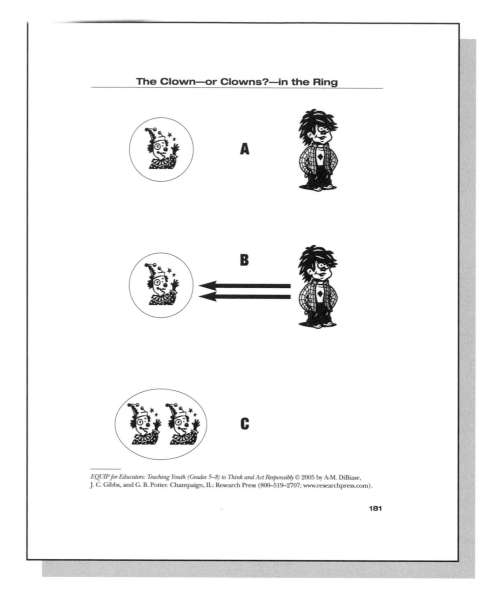

The Clown—or Clowns?—in the Ring

A

B

C

EQUIP for Educators: Teaching Youth (Grades 5–8) to Think and Act Responsibly © 2005 by A-M. DiBiase, J. C. Gibbs, and G. B. Potter. Champaign, IL: Research Press (800–519–2707; www.researchpress.com).

181

Figure 3.1   The Clown—or Clowns?—in the Ring

Note: This figure is based on the work of E. L. Feindler and R. R. Ecton, *Adolescent Anger Control: Cognitive-Behavioral Techniques.* Copyright © by Allyn and Bacon. Adapted by permission.

A: He is a clown and a fool because he is not thinking of all the disadvantages of anger and violence. His goal is to make you a fool, too, to draw you into the circus ring with him.

B: He wants to attach his strings to you. Then he can pull on the strings and draw you into the ring with him.

C: If you let him attach the strings and pull you in, then who is in control? Who is strong? And he wins if you start fighting. How many clowns are there in the ring now?

To apply the example to real life, ask the students:

Has some clown ever succeeded in pulling your strings, pulling you into the ring? What kind of "strings" (e.g., name-calling, challenging you in front of others, making remarks about your family) did you let that person attach to you to pull you into the ring?

Have you ever been a foolish clown, trying to pull someone into the ring with you? What strings did you use to try to make that person into a clown like you?

You can conclude the discussion by inviting the group to list the four benefits of controlling their anger: (a) You won't hurt anybody; (b) Other people will like and help you; (c) You won't get in trouble; and (d) You will feel better about yourself because you will know that you *truly* are strong (truly strong people can control themselves).

Key Role of Mind in Anger, Monitoring Mind and Body, Reducing Anger

OVERVIEW OF EXPECTATIONS AND ACTIVITIES

Students will . . .

♦ Recall the reevaluating and relabeling of anger/aggression from the previous session.

♦ Recognize the components of the "anatomy" of anger.

♦ Assess the early warning signs of anger.

♦ Identify that it is your mind (attitudes, beliefs, what you tell your-self) that makes you angry, not the event "out there."

♦ Apply self-talk reducers that can help them calm down when they are angry (buying time for constructive, socially skilled behavior).

PROCEDURE AND EDUCATOR NOTES

Review Week 1 regarding the benefits of controlling anger and the strength that comes from having options besides fighting. Again, you will be helping the students to step back from anger, this time to examine its working parts and attain some key insights.

Week 2 entails teaching the working parts of the "functional anatomy" of anger. You will be emphasizing the key role of the mind in making the individual angry or in keeping the individual calm.

It is important to emphasize that the mind is the key to emotions and behavior. Accordingly, the group learns to monitor the early warning signs of anger-generating thoughts or attitudes and to replace them with responsible self-talk that reduces anger and buys time for more controlled, constructive behavior to take over.

The acronym used to teach the anatomy of anger is *AMBC:*

A: Activating event

M: Mind activity

B: Body reaction

C: Consequences

It is helpful to use an easel pad to keep track of examples under each heading as the discussion proceeds.
Suggest:

> The activating event, or the *A*, is the thing that can get you angry, that leads up to your anger. These events are also called "hot spots." What are some of your hot spots?

Some categories of examples that might be mentioned by the students are:

> Physical intimidation (bullying you; glaring at you; hitting, pushing, or punching you; putting their hand in your face to make you flinch)

> Verbal insults or threats (putting you down, teasing you, swearing at you, bragging that they can beat you up)

> Unfair demands or accusations (accusing you of something that you did not do)

> The discovery that someone has lied about you (starting a rumor about you)

Skip over the *M* (mind activity), for the moment. Instead, teach the *B* (body reaction) as it relates to the activating event. Ask:

> What do you usually feel or see happening after the activating event, after someone has been punched or put down? What do you think the *B* stands for? *(body reaction)*

> Reactions in your body are early warning signs of anger.

Early warning signs that the students might generate include:

> Fast, shallow, or hard breathing

> Cold, clammy, or sweaty hands

> Tense neck, shoulders, stomach

> Clenched fists

> Gritted or clenched teeth

> Louder or lower voice

> Squinty eyes

> Jittery or light-headed feeling

State:

> You need to be alert and notice when these early warning signs are happening. The last part of our anger illustration is the *C*. What do you think *C* stands for? What is a general word for the results of an activating event like a put-down, followed by, let's say, those body reactions?

You may have to provide the word *consequences*. Examples of such conscquences include threats, fights, making enemies, getting hurt, and getting sanctions like suspensions.
State:

> So that is the *ABC* of anger and aggression. But there is something crucial missing, something we have not covered yet, something that happens between the *A* and the *B*. What does that *M* stand for, do you think?

You may have to provide the words *mind activity*. Then state:

> If you think back to when someone put you down or threatened you, you can usually remember thoughts you had or maybe attitudes, beliefs, or "talk" to yourself that went through your mind and made you angry.

> We call this *self-talk*. You may not even realize you are doing the self-talk until you think about it. What were some of the thoughts you can remember having when you were in a hot spot?

Examples might include "I'm not taking this anymore"; "I'm going to get my respect back"; "I'll get him back"; "I'll teach him"; "I'm getting my way."

> Summarize and emphasize the key point:

> So now we have the *AMBC* of anger and aggression.

> We put the *M* between the *A* and the *B* for a reason. We said *B* stands for body reaction. What is the body reacting to? Is it reacting to whatever event out there happened? Or is it reacting to the meaning you attach to the event, to your thoughts about what the person said or did?

Valuable points emerging from the key point of mind activity may include the following:

How often one is unaware of one's mind activity

How quickly the mind activity or an angry attitude can kick in to cause the body reaction (especially when the activating event has happened many times)

How important it is to become more aware of the thoughts running through one's head so that one can do something about them

Point out the importance of noticing the early warning signs of anger as a signal that one needs to do something about the thoughts that are causing those body reactions. State:

When thoughts in your mind are making you sweat, clench your teeth and your fists, and so on, you are not in control. The other person is the one who is in control because you are letting him pull your strings. Remember the clown in the ring? He is the fool or the one with the problem, and he will keep pulling until there are two fools in the ring: you and him.

So if you do not want to be a fool, you have got to change your mind activity from thoughts that make you start to lose control to thoughts that help you keep your head. What are some calming thoughts you tell yourself?

Have students work in triads to generate some self-talk. Table 3.2 includes sample statements. (This table can be profitably revisited in Week 7, on evaluation.)

Remind the students:

From now on, when you get into a hot spot and notice early warning signs, use these anger-reducing self-talk statements to stay in control.

As a lead-in to the next session, mention that mind activity causing anger usually involves thinking errors, so anger-reducing self-talk will need to include corrections of those errors.

Table 3.2   Talking about Self-Talk: Anger Reducers You Can Use

Before an activating event

Try not to take this too seriously.

Positive mind activity in response to an activating event

Time for a few deep breaths.
Maybe I took it the wrong way.
She would probably like me to get really angry. Well, I'm going to disappoint her.

Self-evaluation

When a conflict is unresolved

It could have been a lot worse.

When a conflict is resolved or coping has been successful

I handled that pretty well.
I thought ahead to the consequence. It worked.

Monitoring and Correcting Thinking Errors

OVERVIEW OF EXPECTATIONS AND ACTIVITIES

Students will . . .

- ◆ Review the anatomy of anger (AMBC) and relate it to the four steps of deescalating anger.

- ◆ Acquire and apply skills for correction of thinking errors.

- ◆ Monitor their thinking errors in daily behavior through self-help logs.

PROCEDURE AND EDUCATOR NOTES

The third week focuses on mind activity, particularly thinking errors. Elicit from students what each letter of AMBC stands for.

Ask what the body reaction (shown in the early warning signs of anger) is a reaction to.

Because anger is caused by the meaning attached to the activating event and not the event itself, the M, or the mind activity, clearly deserves special attention in anger management.

Review anger-reducing self-talk and ask for further examples of students' experiences using these self-statements to reduce anger and help avoid losing control in hot spots.

To introduce the notion that anger-arousing mind activity often involves distortions or errors, suggest the following:

> Who has felt angry waiting in a long line for something you need to do or want to buy?

> You probably thought, "This is unfair. I shouldn't have to wait in this line." But that's an error. Why?

Prompt the students to see that others also have to wait, that they are no exception, and that the thinking error is Self-Centered.

Ask how some of the self-statements learned in the previous session help to reduce anger by correcting various errors in mind activity. For example: "I can't expect people to act the way I want them to" corrects

Thinking Errors

Self-Centered

Self-centered thinking means that you think your opinions and feelings are more important than the opinions and feelings of other people. You may not even consider how another person might feel about things. Self-centered thinking can also mean that you think only about what you want right now and do not think about how your behaviors will affect you or others in the future.

Minimizing/Mislabeling

Minimizing/Mislabeling means that you think your problems or behaviors are not as wrong or harmful as they really are. You put a label on your bad behavior to make it sound okay or good, or you describe someone with a bad name (like *snitch* or *fool*) so it will seem okay to hurt them.

Assuming the Worst

Assuming the Worst means that you think everyone is out to get you (or someone else). *(Example:* If someone accidentally bumps into you in the hall, you assume the person did it on purpose instead of thinking it was an accident.) Assuming the Worst about yourself means that you think only bad things can happen to you and that you can't do anything about it. Assuming the Worst can also mean that you think you or other people will not be able to change or make improvements or do anything about bad things that happen in life.

Blaming Others

Blaming Others means that you do not take responsibility for your own behavior but instead blame other people for harmful behavior when it is really your fault. You may think you can harm innocent others—that they deserve it because people in the past treated you badly. Blaming Others can also mean that you think your bad behaviors are okay because you were on drugs or alcohol or in a bad mood.

the Self-Centered thinking error, as do self-statements that invite perspective taking (e.g., "For someone to be that irritable, he or she must be really unhappy").

To help students learn more about thinking errors typically involved in anger, have the students discuss the John's Thinking Errors exercise (see Figure 3.2). Distribute the exercise and group students in their triads. Have the students complete the exercise in their triads and then reconvene as a whole group to discuss the various students' responses. Emphasize the connection between distorted thinking and violence and, accordingly, the importance of correcting thinking errors before it is too late.

List the students' suggestion as to what thoughts John had (Question 1) and how John should have "talked back" to his erroneous thoughts (Question 3) on an easel pad or in another whole-class format.

Students often become involved in the second part of Question 2, suggesting many possibilities: "He spent her money"; "He beat her"; "He was cheating on her"; "He was drunk all the time"; and so forth.

Organize the students' contributions into the four categories of thinking errors, repeated on the facing page as a reminder. (Post a chart listing the thinking errors where it is clearly visible so students can refer to it.)

Table 3.3 gives examples of each of the four thinking errors and their corrections. The left-hand column represents the web of self-centered rationalizations and other distortions that lead to violence. The right-hand column represents truthful self-talk that reduces anger by correcting those distortions.

Conclude the discussion of John's Thinking Errors by raising Question 4: "If John had corrected his thinking errors, would he have thrown the book at her?" This provides the clincher for fostering the students' realization of the connection between lies and violence and, accordingly, the importance of catching lies and thinking the truth to avoid acting violently. Referring to the John's Thinking Errors exercise can help students be more receptive when you conclude sessions by introducing or examining the self-help logs, described next. These logs are structured devices for helping students to monitor their behavior, thoughts, and feelings.

At this point, introduce the following forms:

Problem Names and Thinking Errors (Figure 3.3)

Self-Help Log A: Problems and Thinking Errors (Figure 3.4)

Self-Help Log B: Positive Behaviors (Structured Version; Figure 3.5)

Self-Help Log C: Positive Behaviors (Open-Ended Version; Figure 3.6)

John's Thinking Errors

Triad members _____ Date _____

John is in the kitchen of his apartment. John's wife, Meagan, is angry at him for something he did to hurt her. She yells at him. She pushes his shoulder. Thoughts run through John's head. John does nothing to correct the errors in his thoughts. John becomes furious. He screams at Meagan. John picks up a book nearby and throws it at her.

1. What thoughts, do you think, ran through John's head, both during the situation and afterward? Suggest some sample thoughts.

2. What are the errors in these thoughts? Remember that Meagan was mad at John because he had done something to hurt her. What do you think that might have been?

3. What might John have told himself in this situation? In other words, how might John have "talked back" to his thinking errors? Suggest some things John could have said to himself to correct each type of thinking error.

4. If John had corrected his thinking errors, would he still have thrown the book?

EQUIP for Educators: Teaching Youth (Grades 5–8) to Think and Act Responsibly © 2005 by A-M. DiBiase, J. C. Gibbs, and G. B. Potter. Champaign, IL: Research Press (800–519–2707; www.researchpress.com).

182

Figure 3.2   John's Thinking Errors

Table 3.3   Analysis of John's Thinking Errors

What John Thought	*What John Should Have Thought*
Self-Centered Who does she think she is?	*Talking back to Self-Centered* I'd be mad, too, if I were her. She has a right to expect better.
Minimizing/Mislabeling I'll teach *her!*	*Talking back to Minimizing/Mislabeling* You don't teach anyone by throwing things.
Assuming the Worst She hates me; it's hopeless; she's going to leave me.	*Talking back to Assuming the Worst* She's mad now, but she still loves me. This isn't the end of the world. If I start treating her better, our relationship will improve.
Blaming Others She was asking for it.	*Talking back to Blaming Others* I started it by treating her unfairly.

Problem Names and Thinking Errors Handout

First provide each student with a copy of the Problem Names and Thinking Errors handout (Figure 3.3), adapted from the work of Vorrath and Brendtro (1985) and Potter, Gibbs, and Goldstein (2001):

> Work through each component of this handout as a whole group, providing sufficient explanation and discussion of each question. Have students complete their own copy of the handout as you progress through your discussion.

> At the end of the group discussion, invite students to share some of their responses to each question.

> Have students retain their copies of this handout.

Self-Help Log A: Problems and Thinking Errors

Self-Help Log A: Problems and Thinking Errors (Figure 3.4) makes it easier for students to remember and report in the sessions. Specifically, it promotes the following in students:

> Self-monitoring of anger/aggression

> Learning what settings are high risk for them and which kinds of problems and thinking errors they are most likely to have

> Evaluating the degree of their anger (correcting Assuming the Worst, or thinking that anger is always hopelessly intense)

> Assessing how well they handle themselves in anger situations

Problem Names and Thinking Errors

Student _____ Date _____

Social/behavioral problems are actions that cause harm to oneself, others, or property.

A. Has someone else's problem(s) ever hurt you?   Yes   No

Think of a time that someone's problem(s) have hurt you. Choose the best name for that problem from the list below and write it here.

_____

B. Have your problem(s) ever hurt someone else?   Yes   No

Think of a time your problem hurt someone else. Choose the best name for that problem from the list below and write it here.

_____

GENERAL PROBLEMS

The first three problems are general problems. These general problems may be related to any of the specific problems. When you use one of the general problem names to describe a behavior, to get a good understanding of the situation you must also name one of the specific problems (Numbers 4–12).

1. Low Self-Image

The person has a poor opinion of himself or herself. Often feels put down or of no worth. Quits easily. Plays "poor me" or perceives self as victim even when victimizing others. Feels accepted only by others who also feel bad about themselves.

Briefly describe a situation in which you or someone you know showed a Low Self-Image problem.

_____

_____

Was a specific problem shown at the same time?   Yes   No

What was the problem?

_____

EQUIP for Educators: Teaching Youth (Grades 5–8) to Think and Act Responsibly © 2005 by A-M. DiBiase, J. C. Gibbs, and G. B. Potter. Champaign, IL: Research Press (800–519–2707; www.researchpress.com).

Figure 3.3   Problem Names and Thinking Errors

Problem Names and Thinking Errors (continued)

2. Inconsiderate of Self

The person does things that are damaging to himself or herself. He or she tries to run from problems or deny them.

Briefly describe a situation in which you or someone you know showed an Inconsiderate of Self problem.

_____

_____

Was a specific problem shown at the same time?   Yes   No

What was the problem?

_____

3. Inconsiderate of Others

The person does things that are harmful to others. Doesn't care about needs or feelings of others. Enjoys putting people down or laughing at them. Takes advantage of weaker persons or those with problems.

Briefly describe a situation in which you or someone you know showed an Inconsiderate of Others problem.

_____

_____

Was a specific problem shown at the same time?   Yes   No

What was the problem?

_____

184   *(page 2 of 7)*

Figure 3.3   Problem Names and Thinking Errors (continued)

Problem Names and Thinking Errors (continued)

SPECIFIC PROBLEMS

4. Authority Problem

The person gets into major confrontations with teachers, parents, and others in authority, often over minor matters. Resents anyone telling him or her what to do or even giving advice. Won't listen.

I know someone who has this problem.	Yes	No
I have this problem.	Yes	No

5. Easily Angered

The person quickly takes offense, is easily frustrated or irritated, and throws tantrums.

I know someone who has this problem.	Yes	No
I have this problem.	Yes	No

6. Aggravates Others

The person threatens, bullies, hassles, teases, or uses put-downs to hurt other people. "Pays back " even when others didn't mean to put the person down.

I know someone who has this problem.	Yes	No
I have this problem.	Yes	No

7. Misleads Others

The person manipulates others into doing his or her dirty work; will abandon them if they are caught.

I know someone who has this problem.	Yes	No
I have this problem.	Yes	No

8. Easily Misled

The person prefers to associate with irresponsible peers, is easily drawn into their antisocial behavior. Is willing to be their flunky—hopes to gain their approval.

I know someone who has this problem.	Yes	No
I have this problem.	Yes	No

(page 3 of 7)   **185**

Figure 3.3   Problem Names and Thinking Errors (continued)

Problem Names and Thinking Errors (continued)

9. Alcohol or Drug Problem

The person misuses substances that can hurt him or her and is afraid he or she will not have friends otherwise. Is afraid to face life without a crutch. Avoids issues and people through substance abuse. Usually is very self-centered and minimizes the use of drugs by saying they are not bad or are within his or her control. When the person does something wrong, he or she blames the drugs by saying, "I was high—I couldn't help it."

I know someone who has this problem.	Yes	No
I have this problem.	Yes	No

10. Stealing

The person takes things that belong to others. Does not respect others. Is willing to hurt another person to take what he or she wants.

I know someone who has this problem.	Yes	No
I have this problem.	Yes	No

11. Lying

The person cannot be trusted to tell the truth or the whole story. Twists the truth to create a false impression. Denies everything when he or she thinks it is possible to get away with it. Finds it exciting to scheme and then get away with a lie. May lie even when there is nothing to be gained.

I know someone who has this problem.	Yes	No
I have this problem.	Yes	No

12. Fronting

The person tries to impress others, puts on an act, clowns around to get attention. Is afraid to show his or her true feelings.

I know someone who has this problem.	Yes	No
I have this problem.	Yes	No

How many problems do you have? _____

What are your most serious problems? _____

186   *(page 4 of 7)*

Figure 3.3   Problem Names and Thinking Errors (continued)

Problem Names and Thinking Errors (continued)

Number 1 problem? _____

Number 2 problem? _____

Number 3 problem? _____

By correctly identifying your problems, you have taken a big step in helping yourself. Save this handout to use later in the program. You may find it very useful.

Thinking Errors

The following terms are used to identify thinking errors. These terms are used throughout the program. When you name your behavioral problem, the thinking error that caused it is also named. *Remember: It is your thinking error that led to your social/behavioral problem.*

THE PRIMARY THINKING ERROR

1. Self-Centered

Self-Centered thinking means that you think your opinions and feelings are more important than the opinions and feelings of other people. Self-Centered is the primary, or basic, thinking error. The Self-Centered thinking error can severely limit one person's consideration for the viewpoint of another person.

Does someone you know seem to have a Self-Centered thinking error? How do you know? Explain without using the person's name.

_____

_____

_____

It is important to understand that a person's thoughts cannot be known by anyone other than that person. You can guess what a person is thinking, but you will not know for sure until that person shares his or her thoughts.

Has anyone ever said to you, "I know what you are thinking," but then was wrong? Explain.

_____

_____

_____

If you want to know what another person is thinking, what do you have to do?

_____

Figure 3.3   Problem Names and Thinking Errors (continued)

Problem Names and Thinking Errors (continued)

SECONDARY THINKING ERRORS

The Self-Centered person uses other (secondary) thinking errors to avoid feeling bad (guilt, remorse, low self-concept) about his or her bad (antisocial) behavior and to allow the selfish thoughts and behaviors to continue. For example, a 17-year-old used a secondary thinking error (Blaming Others) to make himself feel better about breaking into people's homes. He said, "If I started feeling bad, I'd say, 'Tough rocks for him. He should have had his house locked better and the alarm on.'" The Self-Centered person almost always shows his or her basic Self-Centered thinking error *and* one of the following secondary thinking errors.

2. *Minimizing/Mislabeling*

Example: "He was a fool and got jumped." What really happened: "I punched and kicked him because he told his neighbor the truth, that I was the person who stole the neighbor's stereo." Or what really happened: The young man was brutally beaten because he told the principal that someone had a gun and threatened some other kids.

Write another example and explain.

_____

_____

_____

3. *Assuming the Worst*

Example: Someone left a CD player and headphones on the library table. You think that you should take them for yourself because if you don't, someone else will.

Write another example and explain.

_____

_____

_____

Figure 3.3   Problem Names and Thinking Errors (continued)

Problem Names and Thinking Errors (continued)

4. Blaming Others

Example: "I got mixed up with the wrong people." What really happened: You agreed to help your friend take something that belonged to someone else.

Write another example and explain.

_____

_____

_____

Are thinking and behaving connected? Explain.

_____

_____

_____

How many thinking errors do you have? _____

What are your most common thinking errors? _____

Number 1 thinking error _____

Number 2 thinking error _____

Number 3 thinking error _____

By identifying your thinking errors, you have taken a big step in helping yourself to correct faulty thinking. It takes a strong person to admit to thinking errors and the behavioral problems they cause.

Figure 3.3   Problem Names and Thinking Errors (continued)

Considering how they might more constructively cope with such situations in the future

This log lists the 12 behavior problems, along with their underlying thinking errors. Using this vocabulary in problem reporting helps keep the student's attention appropriately focused on behaviors that have harmed others and/or on the reporting of peers' behavior. Just using the vocabulary helps students realize the extent of their antisocial behavior.

Once each of the problems has been named, the student and the educator identify the underlying thinking errors (Self-Centered, Minimizing/Mislabeling, Assuming the Worst, and Blaming Others) and thereby make the problem analysis more penetrating.

To convey these concepts, provide each student with a copy of Self-Help Log A (Figure 3.4).

Discuss each component of Log A as a whole group.

Ask students to complete their own Log A.

Once students have completed Log A, work through each component, discussing the various responses of the students.

Self-Help Logs B and C

Once students are sufficiently advanced in the change process, they may begin completing not only Self-Help Log A: Problems and Thinking Errors, but also Self-Help Log B: Positive Behaviors (Structured Version) and/or Self-Help Log C: Positive Behaviors (Open-Ended Version). These logs are shown in Figures 3.5 and 3.6, respectively. Just as Self-Help Log A assists students in recognizing and monitoring thinking errors, these latter two logs help students recognize and monitor growth in responsible, caring behavior.

When time permits, give each student a copy of Log B: Positive Behaviors (Structured Version). This log helps students apply their knowledge of responsible behavior. Have students fill out the form individually, then discuss responses and student examples as a whole group.

Next provide students with Log C: Positive Behaviors (Open-Ended Version). Students can complete Log C during this session or after another session, whenever you would like students to engage in more self-reflection. Have students fill out this form individually, then discuss examples in the whole group.

Provide students with extra copies of Logs A, B, and C for reference and recording of their future behavior.

Self-Help Log A: Problems and Thinking Errors

Student _____ Date _____

_____ Morning _____ Afternoon _____ Evening

Where were you?

_____ Class _____ Gym _____ Hall _____ In class/session

What kind of problems did you have?

_____ Low Self-Image	_____ Easily Angered	_____ Alcohol or Drug Problem
_____ Inconsiderate of Self	_____ Aggravates Others	_____ Stealing
_____ Inconsiderate of Others	_____ Misleads Others	_____ Lying
_____ Authority Problem	_____ Easily Misled	_____ Fronting

You had this/these problems because of what kind of thinking error?

_____ Self-Centered	_____ Assuming the Worst
_____ Minimizing/Mislabeling	_____ Blaming Others

Describe the problems.

What were you thinking (describe the thinking error)?

How angry were you?

1	2	3	4	5
Burning mad	Really angry	Moderately angry	Mildly angry	Not angry at all

How did you handle yourself?

1	2	3	4	5
Poorly	Not so well	Okay	Well	Great

I will not have this/these problem(s) in the future if I . . . .

_____

EQUIP for Educators: Teaching Youth (Grades 5–8) to Think and Act Responsibly © 2005 by A-M. DiBiase, J. C. Gibbs, and G. B. Potter. Champaign, IL: Research Press (800–519–2707; www.researchpress.com).

190

Figure 3.4   Self-Help Log A: Problems and Thinking Errors

Self-Help Log B: Positive Behaviors
(Structured Version)

Student _____ Date _____

_____ Morning _____ Afternoon _____ Evening

	Yes	No
1. I completed my assigned homework.	___	___
2. I followed the classroom rules.	___	___
3. I contributed to my triad work in class.	___	___
4. I did the assigned work in class.	___	___
5. I accepted constructive criticism.	___	___
6. I stood up for my rights in a positive way.	___	___
7. I accepted responsibility for my actions and did not make excuses.	___	___
8. I talked a peer out of verbally or physically fighting.	___	___
9. I complimented someone for something that person did.	___	___
10. I showed consideration for another.	___	___
11. I _____.		

EQUIP for Educators: Teaching Youth (Grades 5–8) to Think and Act Responsibly © 2005 by A-M. DiBiase,
J. C. Gibbs, and G. B. Potter. Champaign, IL: Research Press (800–519–2707; www.researchpress.com).

191

Figure 3.5   Self-Help Log B: Positive Behaviors (Structured Version)

Self-Help Log C: Positive Behaviors
(Open-Ended Version)

Student _____ Date _____

What did you do to help yourself today?

What did you do to help someone else today?

EQUIP for Educators: Teaching Youth (Grades 5–8) to Think and Act Responsibly © 2005 by A-M. DiBiase,
J. C. Gibbs, and G. B. Potter. Champaign, IL: Research Press (800–519–2707; www.researchpress.com).

Figure 3.6   Self-Help Log C: Positive Behaviors (Open-Ended Version)

To provide a hook into the next anger management session, you can mention that sometimes, in hot spots, anger can build so quickly that by the time one starts to correct one's thinking errors, it is too late—one is already engaged in some conflict. Special techniques for managing such situations will be covered in the next session.

Relaxation Techniques for Reducing Anger

OVERVIEW OF EXPECTATIONS AND ACTIVITIES

Students will . . .

♦ Review cognitive distortions and problem names from the previous session.

♦ Acquire and apply techniques of deep breathing, counting backward, and pleasant and peaceful imagery.

♦ Recognize that the use of relaxation techniques in sudden anger situations can buy crucial time for corrective self-talk and constructive social skills.

PROCEDURE AND EDUCATOR NOTES

A key technique in anger management is engaging in activities incompatible with anger. Especially in these sudden-anger situations, breathing deeply, counting backward, and invoking peaceful imagery are important because they are simpler and therefore quicker, "buying time" for corrective self-talk and constructive social skills to kick in. Students can prevent anger buildup by starting to take deep breaths, for example, even before beginning to deal with thinking errors. State:

> Last week, the technique was corrective self-talk. This week, the techniques pertain to relaxation. These techniques are intended to help deal constructively with anger.

> Relaxation techniques can cut short thinking about an anger-provoking event and can help you keep from becoming angry all over again or thinking about revenge.

> Sometimes, in hot spots, anger can build so rapidly that by the time you start to correct your thinking errors, it is too late—you may find yourself already engaged in violence or aggression.

Review the analysis of John's Thinking Errors (as written in the previous session on the easel pad) by pointing to the *thinking error* and the *talking back* columns, reminding students of the previous week's focus on the importance in anger management of recognizing and correcting one's thinking errors. The review should also include group feedback on students' use of the self-help logs.

Breathing Deeply

Show the value of the first technique—slow, deep breathing—by describing and enacting the example of a basketball player who has just been fouled by an opponent:

> The basketball player is angry at being fouled, and he's nervous because the attention is on him and he needs to make this shot for the team. But he knows he will not make it if he stays angry and nervous. He is at the free-throw line. What does he do? *(Discuss.)*
>
> He probably tries to think calming thoughts, but he also tries to calm down from being fouled by breathing deeply and slowly a few times. You can see him taking those slow, deep breaths. He knows from experience that's one of the best ways to get back in control of the situation. As soon as you start taking a few slow, deep breaths, your body reactions are going to get less angry and nervous, and you're going to have a better chance of making that shot—or, in the situation you're in, doing something responsible rather than destructive.
>
> Now remember to make sure the breathing is slow and deep. "Slow" means that taking in the breath should take 5 or 6 seconds. Hold the breath for a few seconds. Then slowly breathe out, again taking 5 or 6 seconds. Wait a few seconds, then breathe slowly in and out again. It should be a slow rhythm. "Deep" means that your lungs should be full. You will know your lungs are full enough if they are putting some pressure down on the top of your stomach. You should be able to feel that downward pressure.
>
> Okay, let's give it a try. Let's imagine some activating event. What are some things, again, that put you in a hot spot? *(Discuss and write examples on the easel pad.)* Imagine that is happening, whatever it is for you. Now start slow, deep breathing. *(Model deep breathing.)* Could you feel that helping? *(Discuss briefly.)*

Counting Backward

Explain how counting backward can prevent a dangerous buildup of anger:

There are two more things that can come in handy. Another effective relaxation technique is counting backward. You silently count backward (at an even pace) from 20 to 1 when you feel that anger coming on. Sometimes you can just turn away from the hot spot while you are counting. You can count backward as you are breathing deeply. You should use these techniques together to get as much power as you can for regaining control.

Counting Backward plus Slow, Deep Breathing

The next approach combines the two techniques taught previously:

So let's try both of these techniques together. Okay, imagine that worst event. *(Allow 10 to 15 seconds.)* Now get the deep breathing started. *(Model and make sure the students are breathing deeply.)* Now we will count aloud from 20. Now start. *(Model; start counting backward; make sure students are breathing deeply and counting.)* Could you feel that helping? *(Discuss.)* Of course, when you are using this technique, you will be counting silently. *(Lead the students in deep breathing; remind them that they should be counting backward silently.)*

Invoking Pleasant or Peaceful Imagery

In addition to deep breathing and counting backward, pleasant or peaceful imagery will help students calm down:

The third technique you can use is to imagine pleasant or peaceful scenes. You can calm yourself down from angry mind activity by imagining a pleasant or peaceful scene. This is a lot like calming self-talk, except that we are talking about mental pictures instead of thoughts. What are some happy or peaceful scenes you can imagine? *(Through discussion, make a list.)*

All Three Techniques Together

Once students become proficient at these techniques, they can practice using all three at once:

Let's try to see if we can use all three techniques at once. First, think of the activating event that tends to start off the anger-causing self-talk. *(Allow 10 to 15 seconds.)* Now let's start slow, deep breathing. *(Model and make sure students are breathing deeply.)* Now start counting backward from 20, silently. *(Allow 10 to 15 seconds.)* Now imagine your favorite peaceful scene while breathing deeply and counting backward. *(Allow 10 to 15 seconds.)* Could you feel that helping? *(Discuss.)*

These three techniques—slow, deep breathing; counting backward; and pleasant or peaceful imagery—will help you reduce those angry body reactions. If you can, use these three things together for maximum anger-control power. They will buy you crucial seconds; they would have bought John crucial seconds. Then you can start to think straight. You can reduce your anger even more with calming self-talk that corrects your thinking errors.

Encourage students to try these techniques outside the class, letting them know that they will be asked during the next session how their practice went.

Mention that the next session will return to anger-reducing techniques that involve self-talk. In the next session, students will acquire two powerful self-talk techniques for reducing anger.

Powerful Self-Talk Techniques for Reducing Anger: Thinking Ahead to Consequences and Think of the Other Person (TOP)

OVERVIEW OF EXPECTATIONS AND ACTIVITIES

Students will . . .

♦ Review the relaxation techniques from the previous session: deep, slow breathing; counting backward; and pleasant or peaceful imagery.

♦ Review the importance of corrective self-talk for reducing their anger.

♦ Acquire and apply "if-then" thinking ahead to consequences.

♦ Apply the Think of the Other Person (TOP) technique.

PROCEDURE AND EDUCATOR NOTES

After a review of the previous week's relaxation techniques, return to the anger-reducing techniques that involve self-statements.

One of the two self-talk techniques covered in this session has been called "if-then" thinking, or "thinking ahead" (Feindler & Ecton, 1986). Its importance is suggested by the finding that highly aggressive, poorly adjusted children are not as good as other children at anticipating and describing the possible consequences of a completed action for themselves and others.

To develop an awareness of consequences, thinking ahead to consequences includes a discussion of the many ramifications of aggressive or antisocial behavior (immediate and long-term, practical and emotional, for self and for others).

With its emphasis on consequences for others, the discussion naturally leads into a second self-talk technique: Think of the Other Person, or TOP. The perspective taking entailed in TOP is critical for remediating egocentric bias and the Self-Centered thinking errors, the primary cognitive distortion of antisocial children. (For more seriously at-risk students, the TOP strategy is expanded during Week 9 to include the meaning "Think of the pain your actions have caused other people.") The prompts "think ahead" and "TOP" should be presented both as self-statements and as cues for young people to use with one another.

Begin by briefly reviewing the relaxation techniques learned in the previous session and asking the students about their experience with the techniques in the past week. Then introduce thinking ahead:

> Today we are going to get back to self-talk techniques for reducing anger. What self-talk techniques have we learned so far? (*Discuss calming self-talk and, especially, correcting thinking errors.*)
>
> The self-talk techniques for today are very powerful ones. The first one is called *thinking ahead,* or if-then thinking. If I do this negative thing, then that negative consequence will follow, so I'd better not do it.
>
> You can use thinking ahead before you are even in a hot spot—in fact, to prevent one. For example, let's say you are a high school senior and you have a car, and it's in the repair shop. And you know you have had problems in the past when picking up your car at the repair shop.
>
> So now your car is in the shop again, and you can think ahead. You can think, "When I go to pick up my car at the repair shop, it may not be ready." So you are thinking ahead to a consequence right there. And your thinking ahead might result in your thinking of something you can do right now, before you even get to the shop. What's that? (*Discuss telephoning ahead to make sure the car is, in fact, ready.*)
>
> Let's say they said it would be ready, but you remember last time it was not ready. So you can think ahead: What if that happens? How will I feel? (*Discuss feelings of frustration and anger.*)
>
> Okay, but keep thinking ahead. Think of the possible consequences if you lose control because of that anger. Say to yourself, "Think ahead!" Think: If I lose control and blow up and haul off and slug the guy, then they'll call the police. Plus, they'll have my car! So I'd better keep my cool and remember how to express a complaint constructively, to complain in a calm and straightforward way. That's if-then thinking—that's thinking ahead.
>
> Now, in thinking ahead, you have to think of all types of likely consequences. For example, there are not only the first things that happen but also things that are likely to happen later on. So let's say someone is teasing you, and you don't use any skills—you just lose it and beat up the other person. What's the first thing that's likely to happen? (*Discuss the likely immediate consequence—that the person will stop teasing for the moment.*)

But now let's keep on thinking ahead. What else might happen a little later? *(Discuss the likelihood that the other person will try to hit back, will get some of his or her buddies to exact revenge.)*

So chances are, it's not going to end there. So thinking ahead, you've got to think ahead long enough to think of all the consequences because you may not check yourself if you just think of some positive things that might happen first.

So you need to think ahead, both to the first consequences and to later consequences. So far, we've talked about consequences to yourself , but it's also important to consider consequences for the other person.

At this point, write headings for two columns on the easel pad: *Consequences for Self (First and Later)* and *Consequences for Others (TOP: First and Later),* as shown in Table 3.4, Analysis of Consequences. Continue to refer to this chart to organize the following discussion:

This thinking ahead isn't just for anger-type situations. Let's take stealing a car. If I steal a car, chances are I'll get caught, go to court, get sent to jail, and so on.

Even if I don't get caught and go to court, I could get hurt, could get killed in a bad accident.

Can you think of any other consequences for yourself? Maybe some long-run consequences? What has happened in your life after you have done something to hurt others? How have other people treated you after? Have you lost certain friends? Have you gotten a certain reputation you did not really want? Have you lost the respect of some people you care about? *(Discuss.)*

Again, it is very important to think ahead not only to consequences for yourself, but also to consequences for the other person, other people.

Thinking of the other person is so important, in fact, that we have a special name for it: TOP. Remembering TOP will help you stop. If you just think about consequences for yourself, what kind of thinking error is that? *(Discuss Self-Centered thinking errors.)*

TOP means you think about the other person, about the consequences of your actions for others. What hassles will the other person have? If you steal, what hassle will the victim have?

Table 3.4 Analysis of Consequences

	Consequences for Self (First and Later)	Consequences for Others (TOP: First and Later)
General Consequences (other than feelings)	(Discuss first.)	(Discuss second.)
"Feelings" Consequences	(Discuss fourth.)	(Discuss third.)

It may be necessary to engage in special probing for "feelings" consequences for others:

> So how would the other person feel? *(Discuss.)* What about later on—some indirect consequences? When other people who know the victim find out, how will they feel? *(Discuss how the feelings of others are like those peers have had: hurt, angry, confused, panicky, upset, depressed, wanting to get even.)*

> And when the victim breaks the news to his or her family, how do you think they feel? *(Discuss.)*

> What are some more later consequences? Will the person ever be quite the same again? *(Discuss.)*

Finally, probes for "feelings" consequences for the person who steals the car:

> How would you feel if you stole a car? What about in those moments when you are not making *Minimizing/Mislabeling* and *Blaming Others* thinking errors, like saying, "He deserved it"?

> The person did not deserve for you to come along and make him or her a victim. When you are strong enough to face what you are doing and be honest with yourself, you will feel you did a terrible thing to someone, you will feel terrible inside, you will lose self-respect. Have you ever had feelings like that? *(Discuss.)*

> When you tell yourself, "Think ahead," the consequences you are thinking ahead to are all the kinds we have talked about.

> It is important to think ahead to consequences for yourself, but it's especially important to think ahead to consequences for others, to

think "TOP." We are going to have more to say about TOP in a later session.

There is lots to self-talk you can use—not only "Think ahead," but "TOP," "Check yourself," and "Check your thoughts." These self-talk phrases can help you stop behavior that hurts others or yourself before it starts. You can even use them to stop yourself from dwelling on harmful thoughts. *(Discuss.)*

WEEK 6
Achieving Constructive Consequences

OVERVIEW OF EXPECTATIONS AND ACTIVITIES

Students will . . .

- Review if-then thinking (if I do this, then that may happen; thinking ahead to consequences).

- Review the Think of the Other Person (TOP) technique.

- Use "I" statements instead of "you" statements (put-downs and threats) in order to achieve constructive consequences.

PROCEDURE AND EDUCATOR NOTES

In the AMBC anatomy of anger and aggression, *M* (or mind activity) has received most of the attention. In this context, students have learned and practiced several kinds of anger-reducing self-statements: calming, correcting, and if-then thinking (thinking ahead to consequences).

They have also learned to reduce anger through activities with minimal cognitive involvement, such as deep breathing and counting backward.

The *A* and the *B* of AMBC have also been discussed, mainly in terms of the point that the *(B)* body is not reacting directly to the *(A)* activating event, but instead to the *(M)* meaning attached to that event by the mind activity. Week 6 moves the anger management curriculum along to the *C* (Consequences) in AMBC.

Beyond techniques like thinking ahead to consequences, how can students engage in social behavior likely to achieve constructive consequences? Students learn that using the anger-reducing and cognition-correcting techniques enables them to stay calm and think straight. Calm, straightforward thinking enables them to engage in calm, straightforward behavior that leads to constructive rather than destructive consequences.

Students learn to replace "you" statements (put-downs and threats) with "I" statements. Use of this skill is linked with the social skill Expressing a Complaint Constructively, which is taught during Week 1 of the social skills component of the *EQUIP for Educators* program (see chapter 5). This association reinforces the connection between the anger management and social skills components of the curriculum.

The session concludes with a discussion of the difference between making a threat and stating a consequence.

Following a review of the anger "anatomy" learned so far, relate the destructive consequences to "you" statements and explain in contrast how "I" statements typically lead to more positive consequences:

We have been working with the *M* in AMBC. We have also talked about the body reaction and the activating event (hot spot). We said that the body that is getting angry is reacting to what? *(Review the point that mind activity is so crucial because the body reacts directly to that, not to the activating event.)*

But we have not yet directly talked about the *C* in AMBC. *(Review the meaning of* C *in AMBC and stress that an angry mind and body can lead to destructive consequences if not met with the techniques that students have learned.)*

In other words, if you allow yourself to get too upset to think straight, then you are going to start to say some destructive things. There are basically two kinds of destructive things you say when you are angry: put-downs and threats.

For example, let's say you lent someone your radio. Now you want it back, and the person refuses to return it, so when you see the person you say, "Hey, jerk, you'd better give me back my radio if you know what's good for you!" Where was the put-down? Where was the threat? *(Discuss.)*

Put-downs and threats are "you" statements: "You jerk. You'd better do this or else." They are destructive because they attack the other person and provoke a fight. Instead of being *destructive,* we want to be *constructive,* and we do this by replacing "you" statements with "I" statements.

Telling someone how you feel—like "I'm feeling pretty upset about this"— involves an "I" statement. An "I" statement makes a constructive suggestion: I would like you to do this instead.

"I" statements were part of a social skill you learned in Week 1 of the social skills part of this program: Expressing a Complaint Constructively.

If you have been using your anger reducers in hot spots, then you should be calm and straight thinking enough to express yourself in a calm, straightforward way.

Is your tone of voice threatening when you express a complaint constructively?

On the easel pad, recap the following with the students:

Now, the first step in Expressing a Complaint Constructively was to state to yourself what the problem was, how you were feeling about it, and whether you were partly responsible for the problem.

The second step was to make plans for expressing your complaint, like deciding what person you were going to complain to and what you were going to say.

The third step was when you actually role-played Expressing a Complaint Constructively. And there were three things you did as part of that step:

You told the person what the problem was, how you felt about it, and what you would like done about it. For example, if someone has borrowed your radio and still hasn't given it back, you can say, "Joe, you borrowed my radio, and I'm getting upset because it was a while ago. I'd like it back now."

What "I" statements do you hear there? *(Discuss.)* And you say this in what kind of way? *(Discuss calm, straightforward delivery.)*

A final part of the third step said, "If you have contributed to the problem, mention how you may be partly at fault and what you are willing to do."

If you told Joe he could borrow the radio for as long as he liked, you would say as part of that step something like "I know I told you that you could keep it as long as you needed it, but it's been a month now, and I need it back."

What is constructive about this low-key approach? *(Discuss the value of showing that you understand the other person's point of view or encouraging the other person to listen to your point of view.)*

But still, it may not always work. If the other person continues to violate your rights or ignores legitimate points, the nice thing about starting out low-key is that you still have room to gradually firm up your position—without becoming destructive.

You still do not threaten. But you do—in a calm, straightforward way—tell the other person what the consequences will be if the situation is not resolved satisfactorily.

If you say it in a menacing tone of voice, trying to use fear to get your way, you are being threatening, and the other person could be provoked into even worse actions.

To be effective, the consequence should be realistic—something you are willing to carry out.

That is the difference between stating a consequence and making a threat: It's the difference between staying calm and being angry, between saying something realistic and saying something unrealistic.

Modeling

Model using "I" instead of "you" by setting up a hypothetical situation and responding both ways. Use the following example or one that's more relevant to your class:

Let's say that while I was out of the classroom, you made a mess. Then I came back and saw paper all over the room. Listen carefully and see how you feel inside as I talk about my reaction, starting with "you" and then with "I" or "It":

You slobs! You make a mess every time I leave this room. You should be ashamed of yourselves.

Now I'll start talking about my anger using "I" or "It":

It makes me angry to come back and see such a mess in this room. I feel really let down.

Even though both of my responses are about the same thing, did you feel the same each time? How did you feel when I started with "you"? How did you feel when I started with "I"? *(Allow for student response.)*

Point out the following:

When I start with "you," it's like accusing someone. It makes people mad and makes them want to fight back. When I start with "I," I'm saying how I feel and commenting about someone's behavior without putting them down. If I say, "I don't like it when . . ." to a friend, I'm still being a good friend because I'm not putting my friend down. Do you see how the first kind of response leads to destructive consequences? How the second kind of response can achieve a constructive consequence?

Role Play

If there is time, students can break up into triads for role-play practice of giving one another "I" rather than "you" statements in response to some aggravating situation (e.g., one student loaned another student a T-shirt and now finds that the T-shirt has a big hole in it).

Set up some role-play situations in which students have the opportunity to try using "I" statements rather than "you" statements. As role-play situations, use examples of minor conflicts between friends that students suggest.

If you want to give all the students a chance to experience delivering and receiving "you" and "I" statements, ask the students, in their learning triads, to do as follows:

Ask the students to decide who will be A, B, and the observer. Then tell them to imagine that B just tore a hole in a T-shirt B had borrowed from A.

For about 30 seconds have A deliver "you" statements about B and what B did. B should just listen.

Have the observer call "stop"; then have A give the same message, using "I" messages this time.

The observer calls "stop" and repeats the same procedure, but this time B will talk to A about losing a CD borrowed from B.

The first time, B will deliver a "you" message, then an "I" message, as before. A should just listen.

Work through the same process, shifting the observer into the process.

After the exercise, reconvene as a whole group. Ask the students the following questions:

How did you feel when you were delivering a "you" statement?

How did you feel when you were delivering an "I" statement?

Which statement is easier to deliver?

How did you feel when you got a "you" statement?

How did you feel when you got an "I" statement?

Which message is easier to receive?

Self-Evaluation

OVERVIEW OF EXPECTATIONS AND ACTIVITIES

Students will . . .

- Review negative consequences of anger (put-downs and threats).

- Review use of "I" statements instead of "you" statements.

- Use self-evaluation statements (self-reward, constructive self-criticism).

- As a crucial part of self-evaluation, correct thinking errors.

PROCEDURE AND EDUCATOR NOTES

Week 7 moves the anger management curriculum beyond the AMBC model to consider the role of self-statements once an AMBC cycle is completed. Students should already be familiar with self-evaluation, thanks to the self-help logs, which entail both anger rating and identification of thinking errors. (Self-help logs are described in detail in the anger management procedures for Week 3.) The self-reflection required for self-evaluation offers an excellent prelude to the consciousness-raising material encountered in the remaining sessions.

Begin with a review of the previous session, which focused on the *C* of AMBC; then review the way to achieve constructive consequences: by replacing "you" statements or put-downs and threats with "I" statements. Then introduce the main topic of the session.

State:

The anger management skill for today goes beyond consequences—it is something you should do after the consequences, after an incident is over one way or the other. And it is something you have already been doing on your logs: self-evaluation.

Where have you been rating yourself on the logs? *(Discuss the anger and coping behavior evaluations.)*

On the logs, you did only number evaluations. However, you really should do more than just that. If you gave yourself a 4 or a 5 ("well" or "great") for the way you handled yourself in a situation, then give yourself rewarding self-talk, a kind of mental pat on the back: "Hey,

I really kept cool" or "I handled that one pretty well" or "I'm doing better at this all the time."

If you didn't handle the situation well, give yourself constructive feedback on what you can do to handle a situation better the next time: "Next time I'll notice my early warning signs sooner, like my muscle twitch or my angry self-talk."

You may also need to tell yourself other constructive things, like what thinking errors you were making in the situation and what you need to tell yourself next time to talk back to those thinking errors.

Have students form groups of three and instruct the groups to recollect a problem situation, evaluate how the other person in the situation felt, and discuss how they could handle the situation better next time. Discuss how John, after throwing the book, could do a constructive self-evaluation and practice telling himself the truth so that he would not hurt someone again.

State:

Don't mislabel yourself a failure if you don't control your anger perfectly right away. Instead, stay constructive. What would you do differently, and how can you do better next time? Is there any technique you can use from what you've been learning in anger management? *(Encourage student responses.)*

Part of your self-evaluation should be something like this: "These are tough situations—they take time to learn how to straighten out" or "I'll be better at this when I get more practice."

Have the students work in their triads to recollect conflict situations they handled well or poorly and to suggest self-evaluative statements.

WEEK 8
Reversing

OVERVIEW OF EXPECTATIONS AND ACTIVITIES

Students will . .

♦ Review self-evaluation statements (self-reward, constructive self-criticism).

♦ Review self-evaluation and correction of thinking errors.

♦ Discover things they do that make other people angry (realizing how they aggravate others; correcting a Self-Centered error).

♦ Discover what to say to a peer who makes a Blaming Others error (Reversing).

♦ Practice including what they do to others in writing about a conflict (A Story from Two Points of View).

PROCEDURE AND EDUCATOR NOTES

Much of the material in the remaining three anger management sessions is designed to be consciousness-raising, especially as treatment for Self-Centered attitudes in anger and for Blaming Others tendencies generally.

Week 8 shifts the perspective from oneself as the victim of provocations to oneself as a provocateur of others. The focus, then, is on students' tendencies to ignore their own provocations and to blame others totally when they are in fact partly at fault—that is, to make Self-Centered and Blaming Others errors. Each student suggests two things he or she does to aggravate or hurt others, and students practice "reversing" techniques for helping peers who inappropriately blame others.

Begin with a review of the previous week's work, then shift the focus:

This week in anger management, we are going to take a slightly different angle on things. Up until this week, when we have talked about activating events, we have talked about the things other people do to make you angry, the hot spot you are in because of someone else's Aggravates Others problem.

It was always that other person. But someone's got to be that other person; most of us are that other person at least sometimes.

So think about when you are that other person. In fact, if you are that other person a lot more often than you think, what kind of thinking error are you making? *(Self-Centered)*

It is helpful at this point to remind the group of John's situation and review how John ignored what he did to make his girlfriend angry in the first place.

Introduce the Blaming Others thinking error. State:

If you blame the other person when you should be at least partly blaming yourself, what kind of thinking error is that? *(Blaming Others)*

Anger is not just a problem of what others do to anger us and how we should reduce our anger and express a complaint constructively. It is also a problem because of things we do to make other people angry.

We may tend to ignore the times we tease people or threaten them in some way or start rumors about them. This is where your self-evaluation logs can be helpful, to give you a chance to slow down, remember such times, and report when you have aggravated or otherwise harmed someone. (Self-evaluation logs are discussed in detail in the anger management procedures for Week 3.)

So what do you do that amounts to someone else's activating event, someone else's hot spot? What have you done lately, or what did you do in the past?

Have students break from the whole group into their triads for a few minutes and encourage students to discuss their logs with their peers. Reconvene as a whole group and ask students to report on their groups' discussions.

Give each student a copy of the Things You Do That Make Other People Angry exercise (Figure 3.7). Work through the exercise as a group.

State:

As with the self-evaluation that we learned about last week, the aim here is to be constructive. Once you are more aware of how you aggravate others—or how you are partly at fault when others are aggravating you—you are in a position to do something about it.

Things You Do That Make Other People Angry

Student _____ Date _____

List two things you do that make other people angry or two things you have
done that made someone else feel hurt or angry.

1. _____

   _____

   _____

2. _____

   _____

   _____

193

Figure 3.7   Things You Do That Make Other People Angry

How did we say John should talk back to his Self-Centered thinking error? *(Review John's taking his girlfriend's point of view and telling himself the truth: that she has a legitimate right to be upset and expect better treatment.)*

And how did we say that John should talk back to his Blaming Others thinking error? *(Review John's telling himself the truth: that he started the provocations and that grabbing the book was his choice.)*

Now let's say a peer makes a Blaming Others thinking error, not silently but out loud. How would other students "talk back" to the group member to correct that Blaming Others thinking error?

Distribute the Practice Reversing exercise (Figure 3.8) and have the class break into triads to work on it.

The first three thinking error examples are answered for us. *(Discuss.)* What about the next one? What would you say?

Read and discuss each subsequent example. Finally, with the students still in triads, work through the Story from Two Points of View exercise.

A Story from Two Points of View

Begin by telling the students to pretend they have been asked to write an article for a magazine about getting angry. The publisher would like them to make up a story or describe a time when one of their friends did something that made them angry. The article should include a description of how they felt and exactly what they did when the friend made them angry.

After the students write their articles, tell them that the publisher has just called back and said she liked the article. But she also wants to print the full story, including the *other* person's side of the story.

Have each student rewrite the same story from their friend's point of view, explaining why the friend was angry in the first place.

When they have finished, discuss the part of the story that was missing: What the *student* has done to aggravate the friend. Ask: "What were the friend's feelings, besides anger?" and "Is the story more complete now that both sides are included?"

Practice Reversing

Triad members _____ Date _____

Situation 1

A student says:

I don't have any problems. You jerks are the ones with the problem. The only problem I have is you dummies keep hassling me.

You say:

You know, it'll be great when you get the courage to face your problems. Then you'll thank people trying to help you instead of putting them down and blaming them.

Situation 2

A student says:

I got in trouble because both my parents are alcoholics and don't care about me.

You say:

You mean that all people with parents who have problems go out and hurt people?

Situation 3

A student says:

It's all my mother's fault. They never would have caught me if she didn't tell the police I was stealing.

You say:

Did your mother do the stealing? Did anyone force you to steal? No? So whose fault is it, really, that you stole?

Situation 4

A student says:

My friends talked me into it—it's their fault. I just got mixed up with the wrong people.

You say:

_____

_____

EQUIP for Educators: Teaching Youth (Grades 5–8) to Think and Act Responsibly © 2005 by A-M. DiBiase, J. C. Gibbs, and G. B. Potter. Champaign, IL: Research Press (800–519–2707; www.researchpress.com).

(page 1 of 2)

Figure 3.8   Practice Reversing

Practice Reversing (continued)

Situation 5

A student says:

I don't feel like playing basketball. They never pass me the ball.

You say:

_____

_____

Situation 6

A student says:

He was asking for it. He kept teasing me.

You say:

_____

_____

Situation 7

A student says:

I got in trouble because both my parents did drugs and neglected me.

You say:

_____

_____

(page 2 of 2)   **195**

Figure 3.8   Practice Reversing (continued)

Victims and Victimizers

OVERVIEW OF EXPECTATIONS AND ACTIVITIES

Students will . . .

- ◆ Review things they do that make other people angry (realizing how one aggravates others; correcting for a Self-Centered tendency).

- ◆ Review what to say to a peer who makes a Blaming Others error.

- ◆ Develop an awareness of themselves as being the ones who harmed innocent people and develop empathy for victims.

- ◆ (More seriously at-risk students will discuss TOP as "Thinking of the pain your actions have caused other people.")

PROCEDURE AND EDUCATOR NOTES

Week 9 continues to raise consciousness. In the previous session, students became more aware of the ways in which they aggravated others and attempted to escape accountability by blaming others. "Telling themselves the truth" meant admitting to themselves their acts of provocation.

The present session broadens the referent for this awareness from acts of provocation to acts of victimization. The session accomplishes this consciousness raising through use of an empathy-inducing social perspective taking exercise: Victims and Victimizers (see Figure 3.9). This material expands upon not only the previous week but also upon the Week 5 discussion of thinking ahead to consequences for others (TOP).

Consequences for victims are discussed systematically, and emotional consequences are reemphasized. TOP is discussed again, this time as "Think of the pain your actions have caused others" (*at least for more seriously at-risk student groups*).

Students are urged to imagine themselves in the place of their victims. In the discussion of victims and victimizers, the point is made that victimizing others because you were a victim is a Blaming Others thinking error.

The discussion concludes with personal applications, as students come to grips with the extent of their victimization of others.

Victims and Victimizers

Triad members _____ Date _____

You are staying at your grandparents' home for the weekend. Your grandparents have lived in that home for many years. You arrive home with your grandparents from dinner. When you open the front door, you see that the house has been broken into. Many of your grandparents' things have been thrown all around. Their crystal glasses have been smashed. Their family photo album has been destroyed. Some of their things, like a wedding ring that belonged to your great-grandmother, have been stolen.

1. What would be the first thing that you would do?

2. How do you think you would be feeling? Have you ever had anything stolen from you? How did you feel? Does that help you understand how your grandparents feel?

3. Would you leave your grandparents in the house alone for the night? Why or why not? Do you think your grandparents would feel afraid or worried? When have you felt afraid or worried? Does that help you understand how your grandparents would feel?

4. Do you think your grandparents will get their things back?

5. Who are the victims in this situation? Can you think of any long-term or indirect victims? (List some ways that victims suffer: in body, in mind, in money, in daily living, with their friends.)

6. Who are the main victimizers in this situation? If a victimizer were to think ahead to the many ways a victim would suffer, would the victimizer still go ahead and do the crime?

7. Have you ever been made a victim? By whom? Have you victimized others? Whom have you victimized? Do most people who have been victimized go on to victimize others? Which have you been more of, victim or victimizer?

EQUIP for Educators: Teaching Youth (Grades 5–8) to Think and Act Responsibly © 2005 by A-M. DiBiase, J. C. Gibbs, and G. B. Potter. Champaign, IL: Research Press (800–519–2707; www.researchpress.com).

196

Figure 3.9   Victims and Victimizers

Begin with a recapitulation of Week 8, on reversing. Let the group know that this session will provide more ways to take the perspective of others—specifically, of their victims. Ask:

First of all, what is a victim? *(Discuss* victim *as someone who is unfairly hurt by someone else.)*

What is a victimizer? *(Discuss* victimizer *as someone who hurts others, especially someone who unfairly hurts another person or people.)*

We have a good list of victimizing behaviors. *(Refer to the Problem Names, from Week 3.)*

Invite the students to consider a concrete situation involving victims and victimizers.

Distribute copies of the Victims and Victimizers exercise (Figure 3.9) and encourage the students, in their triads, to discuss the questions presented there.

Question 4 is particularly good for stimulating awareness of the permanent psychological harm that can result from victimization.

Consequences to victims are discussed systematically in Question 5; this discussion should be related to the Week 5 discussion of TOP (thinking ahead to consequences for others). Some potential responses to Question 5 are as follows:

In body: Bruised, broken bones, heart attacks, beaten

In mind: Fear, apprehension, insecurity, loss of control over life, loss of concentration, confusion, thoughts of losing life, trauma, anxiety, irritability, guilt, grief over losing something personally meaningful, reliving victimization, lack of trust, emotional problems, paranoia

In money: Loss of job, unpaid bills, loss of money, cost to replace lost or damaged items, medical cost, court cost

In daily living: Loss of sleep, disrupted schedule, can't get to work, loss of appetite, increased stress, health problems

With their friends: Isolation from others, being teased or ignored by others, stress

Question 7 provides an opportunity to broaden the discussion. Suggest:

Remember TOP, from a few weeks ago? Who remembers what TOP stands for? *(Discuss how "think of the other person" is informed by the previous list of ways victims suffer.)*

TOP also stands for something else, something I'll tell you about after we talk about Question 7.

In general, how have you been a victim in your life? From parents, friends, teachers? *(Discuss.)*

Now, how have you been a victimizer? Of your family, friends, teachers, society? *(Discuss.)*

Ask students whether their victims have suffered in some of the ways previously listed.

Do you think most people who have been victims become victimizers? *(Discuss the fact that although some do, many don't.)* So can you use the fact that you have been a victim as an excuse for going out and victimizing others?

Highlight the point that students' own victimization does not mean that they have to victimize others; if that were true, then every victim would become a victimizer. Indicate that such an excuse is a Blaming Others thinking error. One is in effect blaming innocent people for what someone else did.

Which do you think you have been more, a victim or a victimizer? *(Discuss.)*

Continue by expanding the meaning of TOP from "think of the other person" to include "think of the pain your actions have caused other people" (at least for more seriously at-risk students). State:

> TOP also stands for "think of the pain your actions have caused other people." This is self-evaluation on a big scale—evaluating your life, how you have harmed others, where you want to go from here.
>
> Now instead of thinking ahead, you are thinking back. And that is the best way to think ahead to consequences for others—to think back to how your past irresponsible behavior has harmed them.
>
> Imagine yourself as your victim—the pain, how it feels.
>
> Continue to think TOP, to think of the other person and the pain you have caused, to stop yourself before you harm yourself or someone else again.

Have the students form groups of three. Ask them to recollect and record situations in which things would have turned out better if they had thought ahead to how their actions would victimize others. Regroup as a whole class to share situations.

Grand Review

OVERVIEW OF EXPECTATIONS AND ACTIVITIES

Students will...

- ◆ Receive an overall review of the skills they have learned during the previous nine weeks.

- ◆ If time permits, students may practice using these skills in role-play situations.

PROCEDURE AND EDUCATOR NOTES

Guide the students through a review of the key points of anger management:

Session 1: The benefits of managing one's anger for gaining control and having behavioral options

Session 2: The reaction of the body directly to the mind and indirectly to the event

Session 3: The violence stemming from John's thinking errors and corrective self-talk John could have used

Session 4: The use of anger reducers (using calming and correcting self-talk, counting backward, breathing deeply, invoking peaceful imagery)

Session 5: Thinking ahead to consequences (if-then thinking); think of the other person (TOP)

Session 6: The use of "I" statements rather than "you" statements to achieve constructive consequences

Session 7: The importance of self-evaluation

Session 8: Understanding how one does things to make "hot spots" for others; helping one another to correct the Blaming Others thinking error (Reversing)

Session 9: The importance of telling oneself the truth about one's victimization of others

If time remains after the review, have the students break into triads to practice using the skills in combination through role play. Follow the guidelines next presented to conduct the role plays.

Application of Skills to Manage Anger and Correct Thinking Errors: Role Plays

As a whole group, brainstorm some real-life situations that students might encounter in which they could use the controlling anger. (Hypothetical situations are provided at the end of this lesson.)

Have students form groups of three, and select each student to be an A, B, or C.

The As are the main actors, who role-play the anger steps.

The Bs play the instigators.

The Cs coach the main actors through the steps whenever necessary.

Students switch roles in their triads, repeating the role plays with new actors, coactors, and coaches. If you need more ideas, you can use the anger role-play situations described in Table 3.5.

Table 3.5   Anger Role-Play Situations

Friends
1. During a test, a student who sits behind you keeps kicking your chair.
2. You are trying to help someone learn to shoot a basketball, when a peer in your class comes over and starts telling you that you are not explaining it right. The peer tries to take over and explain how to shoot the basketball. You know you have been playing basketball longer and that you are a more experienced player.
3. In the school cafeteria, a student crowds in line and starts shoving you aside. She says you are in her way.

Family
1. You want to watch your favorite TV program, but when you go into the living room, your sister is already watching something else and will not change the channel.
2. Your mother takes you shopping to buy some clothes for you, but she will not let you make any choices for yourself.

School
1. There is a food fight between two kids at your table in the cafeteria. You reach down to pick up a milk carton from the floor. The cafeteria supervisor accuses you of being in the food fight.
2. You turned in your assignment, but your teacher lost it. She said you would have to come after school to make it up.
3. A teacher embarrasses you by criticizing you in front of other students.

Figure 3.10

Educator's Review and Self-Evaluation Form: Anger Management/Thinking Error Correction

Session/Skill _____ Date _____

Triad members _____

In General

☐ Yes ☐ No   1. Did triad members follow the ground rules (concerning listening, confidentiality, etc.)?

☐ Yes ☐ No   2. Were all triad members interested and involved?

                    If no, list the names of uninvolved triad members:

                    _____

                    _____

                    _____

☐ Yes ☐ No   3. Did you find some constructive value in every serious comment made by a triad member?

☐ Yes ☐ No   4. Did you maintain a normal voice volume and speak in a respectful rather than threatening or demanding tone?

☐ Yes ☐ No   5. Did you maintain a balance between criticism and approval by using the "sandwich" style of constructive criticism (in which a critical comment is preceded and followed by supportive ones)?

☐ Yes ☐ No   6. Did you appropriately use the ask, don't tell method?

For the Session

Did you . . .

☐ Yes ☐ No   1. *(After the first session)* Review the previous session's activities and go over students' Self-Help Anger Logs?

☐ Yes ☐ No   2. Use the discussion to continue clarifying the four thinking errors and the 12 social/behavioral problems (e.g., Easily Angered, Misleads Others, Lying)?

EQUIP for Educators: Teaching Youth (Grades 5–8) to Think and Act Responsibly © 2005 by A-M. DiBiase, J. C. Gibbs, and G. B. Potter. Champaign, IL: Research Press (800–519–2707; www.researchpress.com).

Educator's Review: Anger Management/Thinking Errors (continued)

☐ Yes ☐ No   3. Use the easel pad or another whole-class format to record the main points of the session and triad members' responses?

☐ Yes ☐ No   4. If applicable, remind triad member to fill out self-help logs: for problems and thinking errors (Self-Help Log A) and for positive behaviors (Self-Help Logs B and C)?

☐ Yes ☐ No   5. Did you generally keep the overall discussion a step back from the students' personal problems?

☐ Yes ☐ No   6. Monitor/elicit/reward any recognition that anger is the product of one's thoughts?

☐ Yes ☐ No   7. Monitor/elicit/reward the use of self-talk techniques?

☐ Yes ☐ No   8. Monitor/elicit/reward recognition of the feelings of and/or harm done to another person?

CHAPTER
4 EQUIPPING WITH SOCIAL SKILLS

The term *social skills* typically refers to balanced and constructive behaviors in difficult interpersonal situations. A student who deals with negative peer pressure by suggesting a constructive alternative activity illustrates the use of social skills, as does the student who calmly and sincerely offers clarification or apologizes to an angry accuser. Social skills are crucial for social action.

Anger management preceded this chapter on social skills for a reason: It does not do much good to teach students social skills if they do not first know how to manage their anger. But once they can keep a level head, they will still need to learn and practice handling difficult social situations in a balanced and constructive manner. In other words, your at-risk students probably have social skills deficiencies that must also be remedied if they are to continue their progress toward responsible thinking and acting. As Cleveland school teacher Dewey Carducci (1980) observed, at-risk students typically do not know what specific steps are necessary in a difficult situation to resolve it constructively. Rather than being balanced and constructive, the responses of these youths are typically imbalanced in favor of their own immediate perspectives; their failure to see other points of view is obvious as they spew forth threats against others and put them down with insults. Carducci's reference to "steps" reflects the revolutionary idea in psychoeducation first proposed by our late (and sorely missed) colleague Arnold P. Goldstein: Why not break the skills of responsible social interaction down into concrete, manageable steps? Why not have students see, try, and practice these steps until social skills (like any other skills) come naturally to them?

Teaching the steps involved in social skills or balanced and responsible interpersonal behavior is the focus of this chapter. The 10 social skills comprising this component of the *EQUIP for Educators* curriculum, listed by week in Table 4.1, address the deficiencies most in evidence among at-risk students (see Goldstein, Glick, & Gibbs, 1998). Many of these students could also benefit from remediation in a wider range of social-behavioral areas, however. If you have sufficient time and

Table 4.1 The 10-Week Format for Equipping with Social Skills

Week 1	Expressing a Complaint Constructively (Skill 1)
Week 2	Caring for Someone Who Is Sad or Upset (Skill 2)
Week 3	Dealing Constructively with Negative Peer Pressure (Skill 3)
Week 4	Keeping Out of Fights (Skill 4)
Week 5	Helping Others (Skill 5)
Week 6	Preparing for a Stressful Conversation (Skill 6)
Week 7	Dealing Constructively with Someone Angry at You (Skill 7)
Week 8	Expressing Care and Appreciation (Skill 8)
Week 9	Dealing Constructively with Someone Accusing You of Something (Skill 9)
Week 10	Responding Constructively to Failure (Skill 10)

opportunity, we recommend that you supplement the core skills presented in this chapter with additional social skills useful in primary and secondary prevention (see Goldstein, 1999; McGinnis & Goldstein, 1997).

FOUR PHASES OF SOCIAL SKILLS LEARNING

Like many other skills (bicycle riding, boxing, swimming, playing a musical instrument, etc.), social skills are typically learned in the context of four phases (see Table 4.2). These four phases (following an introduction to the skill being taught) constitute the teaching format for each of the 10 sessions in the social skills component of *EQUIP for Educators*.

To introduce each social skill at the beginning of each session, follow these steps:

1. Announce the social skill to be modeled and practiced.

2. Distribute copies of the appropriate skill steps (cards or sheets on which you have printed the skill name and steps). You will also need to write the skill steps on an easel pad or use another whole-class format.

3. Read the list of suggested situations and discuss other situations in the students' experience in which the skill would have helped.

4. Ask a student to read the steps of the given skill aloud as others read along silently.

5. Break the group into their designated triads. (See chapter 2 for discussion of a procedure for forming triads.)

Table 4.2   Four Phases of Social Skills Learning

> ***Phase 1: Showing (Modeling) the Skill***
> Acquiring some notion of the skill
>
>
>
> ***Phase 2: Trying the Skill (Enactment)***
> Attempting to perform the skill by imitating or role-playing what was modeled
>
>
>
> ***Phase 3: Discussing the Skill (Feedback)***
> Gaining feedback on the attempt and thereby improving performance
>
>
>
> ***Phase 4: Practicing the Skill***
> Refining the improved performance and consolidating it into a habit; generalizing the habit by practicing it in increasingly diverse and challenging contexts

For trying and discussing the skill, each student should do as follows:

1. Select an appropriate situation (from personal experience or from the list of suggested situations) and describe it to the other members of the triad.

2. Select a partner (who will be needed in the latter steps of the skill).

3. Decide which peer in the triad will provide feedback on which step of the skill.

As students conduct this process, walk around the room among the triads, offering guidance or responding to questions.

At the conclusion of each session, have students reconvene in the group as a whole. Elicit a general discussion of the role-play experience and distribute copies of the Social Skills Practice Sheet (see Figure 4.1). At this point, you may wish to solicit the group's thoughts on consequences for group members who do not complete the practice sheet.

We need to say more about showing the skill (modeling), trying the skill (enactment), discussing the skill (feedback), and practicing the

Social Skills Practice Sheet

Student _____ Date _____

Practice assignment

Skill _____

If applicable:

Use with whom? _____

Use when? _____

Use where? _____

Describe what happened when you did the practice assignment. For example, did you skip any steps? What was the other person's reaction?

_____

_____

_____

Rate yourself on how well you used the skill. (Check one.)

___ Excellent   ___ Good   ___ Fair   ___ Poor

EQUIP for Educators: Teaching Youth (Grades 5–8) to Think and Act Responsibly © 2005 by A-M. DiBiase, J. C. Gibbs, and G. B. Potter. Champaign, IL: Research Press (800–519–2707; www.researchpress.com).

197

Figure 4.1   Social Skills Practice Sheet

skill. Before undertaking these phases, however, we must introduce students to the idea of learning social skills.

INTRODUCING SOCIAL SKILLS

Before beginning instruction in the first skill, introduce the idea of learning social skills and explain to the students the importance of practicing those skills. Label role-play activity in appealing terms. Suggest:

> How do you learn any skill? How did you learn to ride a bicycle? Swim? Play basketball? *(Discuss briefly.)*
>
> Well, social skills are no different. Dealing constructively with negative peer pressure or with someone who angry at you, or even caring for another person, is a skill. We will be using the following four phases in learning social skills. *(Write the four phases on the easel pad.)*
>
> 1. Seeing someone doing the skill *(showing)*
>
> 2. Trying to do what you saw *(trying)*
>
> 3. Finding out what you did right and wrong and how you can do better *(discussing)*
>
> 4. Practicing the skill and seeing improvement *(practicing)*
>
> Role-playing is critical in learning a social skill. In some parts of the role play, you will even be talking out loud to try out the thinking that you will do silently later as you practice.

This general introduction should take approximately 10 minutes. In subsequent weeks, begin each new skill by reviewing students' practice on the previous session's skill, as reflected on their Social Skills Practice Sheets. Elicit students' self-evaluation ratings from the practice sheets and encourage reporting of successful outcomes.

SHOWING THE SKILL (MODELING)

Once the group has assigned responsibilities for feedback and read the skill steps, model the skill with an assistant (a student or another adult) to prepare students to conduct their own role plays. Remind students that the first step in learning any skill is usually watching someone else do it. Indicate that feedback on each student's performance of each step will be expected from the designated students in a triad.

Remind students that showing (and trying) the skill will often involve thinking aloud. Suggest:

Normally, we would think inside our heads, silently. Thinking out loud is like any other skill. At first it doesn't feel natural, and you have to do some artificial things to get the hang of it, but gradually, with practice, it becomes part of you and does feel natural. Then you do it automatically, without thinking out loud or thinking much at all about the steps.

In preparation for discussion of the skill, elicit from the students comments about the respective steps: "How did I do? For example, Step 1?" And so on.

Your response should model social skills for the students, especially students who show off by putting down your performance. For example, you might say, "I'm sure my role play could have been better, and I'd like to know specifically what to work on."

By remaining constructive, you encourage the students to give up on power games and enter into the enterprise of learning the social skills.

TRYING THE SKILL (ENACTMENT)

After your modeling demonstration of the social skill, each student in the triads takes a turn role-playing the skill. (Students rotate the role of providing feedback to triad members as well.)

Remind students that the next step after showing the skill is trying the skill, so it is their turn now.

First, group members must think of situations in which they might need the skill (or make use of the sample situations provided).

Within their triads, students must decide on a partner for role play. The students not participating in the role play are reminded to provide feedback.

Instruct students to refer to the skill steps written on an easel pad that students can readily see, or on individual skill cards listing the steps.

Students should take turns volunteering to role-play the social skill.

Before beginning, each role player should describe the situation. The description should include the physical setting, the events immediately preceding the role play, and the actions the coactor should display.

During the role plays, visit the different triads to provide whatever help, coaching, and encouragement the actors need to keep the role play following the prescribed steps. The student in the triad who has the role of providing the feedback should do likewise.

The role-playing parts should be alternated in each session so that each student frequently plays the different roles with different situations.

DISCUSSING THE SKILL (FEEDBACK)

After each social skill role play, students provide feedback on the performance of each step.

Encourage the student to support the coactor and to provide feedback.

For the primary person in the role play: "How well was the step followed?"

The feedback should be honest: "_____ needs to know what he/she should work on improving in the follow-up practice."

Although the social skill steps have been formulated to apply to as wide a variety of situations as possible, some elements of some steps may not be applicable to some situations proposed for the role plays; by the same token, some situations may require elaboration of some of the steps if constructive social action is to be accomplished. In these instances, the teacher and the students may work together to modify the steps.

PRACTICING THE SKILL

When students have completed their role plays and received feedback, they plan for follow-up practice using the Social Skills Practice Sheet. Such constructive social behavior among students yields the additional dividend of contributing to the development of a positive culture.

While distributing the practice sheets, remind the students that one cannot learn any skill without practicing it.

For the specific social skills, steps are defined for students to work through in their triads. The information in italics is intended for the facilitator (teacher, leader) to emphasize to the students in whole-group discussion of the skill steps, prior to students' dispersing into their triads for role plays. Points may be revisited when triads reconvene as a whole group.

AFTER THE SESSION

After the session, review the session and your role as educator. Evaluate your effectiveness in terms of the four phases by filling out an Educator's Review and Self-Evaluation Form (Social Skills) for each working triad. A reproducible copy of this form is given as Figure 4.5, at the end of the chapter.

WEEK 1
Expressing a Complaint Constructively

STEP 1: IDENTIFY THE PROBLEM

♦ How are you feeling? What is the problem? Who is responsible for it? Did you contribute—or are you contributing—to the problem in any way?

Discuss how you can recognize a problem: by how someone treats you or what the person says to you; by the way you act toward someone or what you say to the person; by the way you feel inside.

STEP 2: PLAN AND THINK AHEAD

♦ To whom should you express your complaint? When? Where? What will you say?

Discuss when it is a good time to tell that person—when the person is not involved with something else or when the person is alone and seems calm. Advise students to wait until they have calmed down before approaching the person.

> **For Steps 3 and 4, the student will need a partner.**

STEP 3: STATE YOUR COMPLAINT

♦ Greet the person in a friendly way.

♦ Calmly and straightforwardly, tell the person the problem and how you feel about it.

♦ If you have contributed to the problem, mention how you may be partly at fault and what you are willing to do.

Point out that if the person gets angry, you can talk about the problem some other time. The person is less likely to get angry if you are strong enough to apologize for your role in the problem.

STEP 4: MAKE A CONSTRUCTIVE SUGGESTION

♦ Tell the person what you would like done about the problem.

◆ Ask the other person if he or she thinks your suggestion is fair.

◆ If the *other* person makes a constructive suggestion, say that you appreciate the suggestion or that it sounds fair.

Students can mention how their suggestion would help the other person, too. To help clear up any remaining hard feelings, students may wish to ask the person how he or she feels about the suggestion.

SUGGESTED SITUATIONS FOR USING THIS SKILL

1. The teacher gives you an assignment that seems too difficult for you.

2. Your friend usually chooses what the two of you will do.

3. Your friend has spread a rumor about you.

4. You just bought a pair of running shoes and left the store, and now you realize the salesperson shortchanged you.

5. You share a room at home with your brother, who is always using your things without asking you.

6. Your parents will not let you go to a movie with a friend.

7. Your teacher keeps giving you work that is too easy. It's the same work over and over again, and you are really bored.

8. Your brother is gone, and now your parents are making you do his chores, too.

WEEK 2
Caring for Someone Who Is Sad or Upset

STEP 1: OBSERVE THE PERSON

- ◆ Does he or she look or sound sad? Upset? How strong might the feelings be?

Participants will need to pay attention to signs that the person may be sad or upset—hunched-over posture, expression on face, tone of voice.

STEP 2: PLAN AND THINK AHEAD

- ◆ Ask yourself: Should I walk over to the person? Now? Or later?

Emphasize that if the person seems very angry or upset, it may be best to wait until the person has calmed down.

> **For Steps 3 and 4, the student will need a partner.**

STEP 3: START A CONVERSATION

- ◆ Walk over to the person. Say something like "What's up?" "How are you feeling?" "Want to talk about it?"

STEP 4: LISTEN AND "BE THERE"

- ◆ Listen to what the person says.
- ◆ Encourage him or her to talk.
- ◆ Let the person know you will be around if he or she wants to talk some more about it or if there is anything you can do.

SUGGESTED SITUATIONS FOR USING THIS SKILL

1. A classmate has been teased a lot lately.

2. A friend's family member has been ill.

3. Your mother or father is slamming doors and muttering to himself/herself.

4. A friend hasn't been chosen for a game, or a classmate just watches a game instead of asking to join.

5. A friend tells you that her new sneakers have just been stolen.

6. Your brother or sister just failed a major examination.

7. Your closest friend just found out that his parents are getting separated.

EDUCATOR NOTES

Be particularly alert to provide coaching in Step 4, Listening. Many students will move right into giving advice or suggestions, having scarcely listened. Emphasize at the outset how important it is just to listen and restrict what you say to words that will encourage the person to elaborate on his or her feelings. Stress the importance of being available.

You may want to use supplementary checklists for this exercise: Keys to Good Listening (Figure 4.2) and Nonlistening Behaviors (Figure 4.3). Triad members serving as feedback providers can complete the form titled How Well Did You Listen? (Figure 4.4).

Keys to Good Listening

Student _____ Date _____

1. Look at the person.

2. Let the person finish speaking.

3. Say something to show you are listening.

4. Give a brief encouragement.

   Yeah.

   Really?

   Hmm.

   Wow!

   Cool!

5. Ask a question to show you would like to know more.

   What happened next?

   How did you do that?

   Where did you go?

   What did you do then?

6. Sum up what the person is saying.

   It sounds like you . . . .

   From what you said, it seems that . . . .

   So you think that . . . .

   In other words, you . . . .

EQUIP for Educators: Teaching Youth (Grades 5–8) to Think and Act Responsibly © 2005 by A-M. DiBiase, J. C. Gibbs, and G. B. Potter. Champaign, IL: Research Press (800–519–2707; www.researchpress.com).

198

Figure 4.2   Keys to Good Listening

Nonlistening Behaviors

Student _____ Date _____

1. Changing the subject

2. Trying to make a joke out of something

3. Giving advice

4. Ignoring or fidgeting

5. Not looking at the speaker

6. Turning your body away from the speaker

7. Laughing inappropriately

8. Interrupting by saying things like "You think that's great, you should hear what I did," or "That reminds me of the time . . . ."

9. Looking bored

10. Saying, "Yeah, Yeah, Yeah," as if you want the speaker to hurry

11. Playing with paper or other things

EQUIP for Educators: Teaching Youth (Grades 5–8) to Think and Act Responsibly © 2005 by A-M. DiBiase, J. C. Gibbs, and G. B. Potter. Champaign, IL: Research Press (800–519–2707; www.researchpress.com).

199

Figure 4.3   Nonlistening Behaviors

How Well Did You Listen?

Student _____ Date _____

Put a check mark next to the things you did while you were listening.

_____ I sat quietly while the speaker was talking.

_____ I ignored the distractions.

_____ I faced the speaker.

_____ I watched the speaker's expression.

_____ I thought about what the speaker was saying and not just about what I wanted to say.

_____ I nodded my head now and then to show I was interested in what the speaker was saying.

_____ I made little comments to show I was listening.

_____ I asked questions to encourage the speaker to tell me more.

_____ I let the speaker finish talking before I asked a question.

_____ I summed up what the speaker said.

One of the things I could have done a little better is _____.

EQUIP for Educators: Teaching Youth (Grades 5–8) to Think and Act Responsibly © 2005 by A-M. DiBiase, J. C. Gibbs, and G. B. Potter. Champaign, IL: Research Press (800–519–2707; www.researchpress.com).

Figure 4.4   How Well Did You Listen?

After the negative pressure has been established, have the observer in each triad freeze the role play for Steps 1 and 2.

STEP 1: THINK, "WHY?"

- ◆ Think about what the other person is saying.

- ◆ What is it the person wants you to do? Why does the person want you to do it?

STEP 2: THINK AHEAD

- ◆ Think about the consequences if you do what the person wants you to do. Who might get hurt?

- ◆ How might you feel if you go along?

- ◆ How *should* you feel if you go along?

> **For Steps 3 and 4, the student will need a partner.**

STEP 3: DECIDE WHAT YOU SHOULD DO

- ◆ What reasons will you give the person?

- ◆ What will you suggest to do instead?

Instruct students to continue the role play.

STEP 4: TELL WHAT YOU DECIDED

- ◆ In a calm, straightforward way, tell the person what you have decided.

- ◆ Give a good reason—for example, how the pressure makes you feel or who might get hurt if you do what the person wants.

If more than one person is involved in the negative pressure, encourage students to tell their decision to one person in the group. Giving a good reason for not going along may help the members of the group rethink what they should do.

STEP 5: SUGGEST SOMETHING ELSE TO DO

This should be something still enjoyable, but responsible.

SUGGESTED SITUATIONS FOR USING THIS SKILL

1. A peer is teasing someone or planning to take something that belongs to someone else, and they want you to join in.

2. A group of peers are planning to vandalize a neighborhood and want you to come along.

3. Some of your friends decide not to go back to school after lunch, and they want you to come along with them.

4. A group of peers ask you to join them in giving the substitute teacher a difficult time.

EDUCATOR NOTES

Indicate to students that this social skill is a crucial tool in helping them avoid an Easily Misled problem. It is also important to stress that blaming irresponsible behavior on negative peer pressure involves a Blaming Others thinking error.

Note also the use in Step 2 of thinking ahead to consequences (TOP), discussed as part of the anger management component of the program (see chapter 3).

Keeping Out of Fights

STEP 1: STOP AND THINK ABOUT WHY YOU WANT TO FIGHT

Tell students that, if they need to, they can breathe deeply, count backward, or think calming thoughts to calm down. They can also consider whether they did anything to contribute to the problem.

STEP 2: THINK AHEAD

- Ask yourself, "If I fight, then what will be the consequences?"

Encourage students to remember to think about consequences for others (TOP), including people who are not on the scene but who will be affected later on: How will they feel? What will they do? How will you feel? What are the likely consequences later on for you?

> **For Step 3, the student will need a partner.**

STEP 3: THINK OF A WAY TO HANDLE THE SITUATION BESIDES FIGHTING AND DO IT

- Should you walk away for now?
- Give a displeased look?
- Talk to the person in a calm and friendly way?
- Ask someone for help in solving the problem?

Ask triad members: "Is the other person calm enough or reasonable enough to talk to?" "Are you calm enough yet to talk?" "Who might help you resolve the situation constructively (teacher, parent, friend)?" Point out that in some situations, such as self-defense or the defense of some other victim, you may have no choice but to fight.

SUGGESTED SITUATIONS FOR USING THIS SKILL

1. A peer has just come up to you and demanded you give him your CD player.

2. You just found out who stole your running shoes.

3. A peer starts teasing you and calling you names.

4. You lost your privilege to participate in a class field trip because someone told your teacher you spray painted on the outside of the school building, and you just found out who told on you.

5. A peer takes part of your lunch and drops it on the floor.

6. In a baseball game, you have just come up to bat. The other team's pitcher yells that you can't hit the ball and calls you a bad name.

7. You are shooting baskets in physical education class with your new basketball. A peer comes up and steals your ball and says it's hers now.

EDUCATOR NOTES

If an occasion does not arise for practicing the skill, students may be given the option of completing the Social Skills Practice Sheet with information from a past incident. Note the use in Step 2 of thinking ahead, TOP techniques.

WEEK 5
Helping Others

STEP 1: THINK, "IS THERE A NEED?"

◆ Decide if the other person might need or want your help.

Students will have to think about the needs of the other person: "What is the person doing or saying, or what is happening, that makes you think the person needs help?"

STEP 2: THINK OF HOW YOU CAN HELP

◆ Which way would be best?

Encourage students to ask: "Does the person need something done? Need someone to listen? Need to hear words of encouragement?" "Should someone else help?"

For Steps 3 and 4, the student will need a partner.

STEP 3: PLAN AND THINK AHEAD

◆ Ask yourself, "Is this a good time for me to offer help?"

Students should ask themselves whether the person could use the help better later on. If so, the students will need to be sure they are not supposed to be doing something else at the time they offer help.

STEP 4: OFFER TO HELP

◆ Ask the other person, "Need some help?" or "Want some help?" or go ahead and offer to help in some way.

◆ If the other person says yes, follow through with the help.

Stress that it is important to make the offer sincerely, allowing the other person to say no if he or she does not really want help. Indicate that students should not feel hurt or offended if the person says no or asks someone else for help. If they do help, they should ask themselves how they feel when they give the help. Point out that helping one another is what the group should be all about.

SUGGESTED SITUATIONS FOR USING THIS SKILL

1. A sick friend needs to keep up-to-date with schoolwork.

2. The person sitting next to you is having difficulty with his math questions.

3. Your teacher needs help arranging chairs in the classroom.

4. Your brother is probably not going to finish his chores in time before your mother comes home.

5. Your neighbor is elderly and cannot shovel his driveway. There has just been a snowstorm.

6. Your friend forgot her lunch at home.

EDUCATOR NOTES

It is important to help students understand that sometimes helping people means doing something against their wishes—for example, students must learn to say no if helping requires them to break the law or hurt others.

WEEK 6
Preparing for a Stressful Conversation

> **The student does not need a partner for this skill.
> Instead, the student explains the situation to the other
> two students in the triad.**

STEP 1: IMAGINE YOURSELF IN THE STRESSFUL SITUATION

- ◆ How will you feel at the start of the stressful situation?

- ◆ Who is responsible for the situation?

STEP 2: IMAGINE THE OTHER PERSON IN A STRESSFUL SITUATION

- ◆ How might the other person feel at the start of the stressful situation? Why?

Students might feel tense, anxious, defensive, impatient, and so on. (This step is related to the TOP self-talk.)

STEP 3: PLAN WHAT TO SAY

- ◆ Practice saying it in a calm, straightforward way.

Tell students that if they can think of any way they have been contributing to the stressful situation, they can mention that while practicing saying what they want to say.

STEP 4: THINK AHEAD TO HOW THE OTHER PERSON MIGHT FEEL

- ◆ What might he or she say in response to what you will say?

Ask students: "Will the other person respond constructively to what you plan to say? If not, can you think of anything better to say?"

SUGGESTED SITUATIONS FOR USING THIS SKILL

Preparing to ask for something important or to seek some important goal in the conversation:

1. You have an appointment tomorrow to talk to your school's basketball coach about trying out for the team. She is known to be tough.

2. You need to talk to your teacher about a test you failed.

3. You want to talk to your teacher to explain a fight that you were in after school on school grounds.

Preparing to reveal or explain something upsetting to someone:

1. You have been caught spray painting the school building, and you know you are going to have to speak to the principal about it.

2. You have to go talk to your teacher to discuss an earlier incident in which you had been disrespectful to her.

3. You have to telephone your parent this afternoon and say that you got into a fight and may be suspended.

EDUCATOR NOTES

No partner is needed for the role play because this social skill is restricted to preparation. Note the use of thinking ahead (TOP; anger management, especially in Step 4). Students can, however, discuss their thoughts about each step in their learning triads.

WEEK 7
Dealing Constructively with Someone Angry at You

The student needs a partner in all steps of this skill.

STEP 1: LISTEN OPENLY AND PATIENTLY TO WHAT THE OTHER PERSON IS SAYING

◆ Nod your head or say, "mm-hmm."

◆ If you need to, ask the angry person to tell you specifically what things you said or did that made him or her upset.

Stress that it is important not to interrupt or fidget. If students feel themselves getting angry, they can breathe deeply or tell themselves to stay calm. Ask them to put themselves in the angry person's place (TOP) and remember that defending themselves at this point will only make the person angrier.

STEP 2: TELL THE PERSON YOU UNDERSTAND WHY HE OR SHE IS UPSET OR THAT HE OR SHE HAS A RIGHT TO BE ANGRY

◆ Think of something you can agree with—say that the person is right about that.

If students cannot agree with any part of what the person is saying, they can agree that they do sometimes make mistakes or hurt people and that they regret this when it happens.

STEP 3: APOLOGIZE OR EXPLAIN

◆ Make a constructive suggestion to correct the problem.

Tell students that if they are mainly at fault, then they will need to apologize for the hurt they caused and say that they plan to do better (and mean it).

SUGGESTED SITUATIONS FOR USING THE SKILL

1. Your teacher is angry with you because you were disruptive during class.

2. Your parent is angry about the mess you have left the house in.

3. Your friend is angry that you called him a name.

4. A classmate has just gotten a week's detention. You started the fight that made this happen, and the person is very angry with you.

5. Some members of your team are angry with you because you fouled an opposing player, the player scored, and your team lost the basketball game.

6. Your parent is angry at you because he or she just heard you complain to your brother that your supper tastes disgusting.

7. Your friend is angry with you because she let you borrow her new sneakers for physical education class and you wore them outside and ruined them in the mud.

WEEK 8
Expressing Care and Appreciation

STEP 1: THINK, "WOULD THE OTHER PERSON LIKE TO KNOW I CARE ABOUT AND APPRECIATE HIM OR HER?"

♦ How will the person feel?

Explain that the other person may become embarrassed or may feel good.

STEP 2: PLAN AND THINK AHEAD

♦ What will you say? When and where will you say it?

Point out that it is often easier to express care and appreciation when others are not around.

> **For Step 3, the student will need a partner.**

STEP 3: TELL THE PERSON HOW YOU FEEL IN A FRIENDLY MANNER

SUGGESTED SITUATIONS FOR USING THIS SKILL

1. You thank a teacher for something he or she has done.

2. You tell your parents that you love them.

3. You tell your friends that you like them and want to continue being friends.

4. A close friend has helped you work out a serious problem.

5. You have made a great deal of progress in your reading. Your sessions with the resource teacher are finished and you want to thank the teacher.

6. Your mother has just given you a new coat for your birthday.

7. Your grandmother, who spent time raising you, is very sick. You are visiting her in the hospital.

8. You are leaving your summer camp after the entire summer, and you have to say goodbye to a friend who has become very close to you.

Dealing Constructively with Someone Accusing You of Something

STEP 1: THINK, "HOW DO I FEEL?"

♦ If you are upset, stop and say to yourself, "I have to calm down."

If necessary, students can also use other anger reducers, such as taking a deep breath or counting to 10. If the other person is very angry, students can tell the person that they understand how he or she feels or that he or she has a right to be upset.

STEP 2: THINK, "WHAT IS THE OTHER PERSON ACCUSING ME OF? IS HE OR SHE RIGHT?"

Explain that it is important to be honest with yourself about the situation. This step amounts to using TOP. Two responses are possible: One if the accuser is right, the other if the accuser is wrong.

> **For Step 3, the student will need a partner.**

STEP 3: IF THE ACCUSER IS RIGHT—IN A CALM, STRAIGHTFORWARD WAY, SAY YOU ARE SORRY.

♦ Offer to make up for what happened or say you will not do it again.

ALTERNATIVE STEP 3: IF THE ACCUSER IS WRONG—IN A CALM, STRAIGHTFORWARD WAY, TELL THE ACCUSER THAT WHAT HE OR SHE SAID IS NOT TRUE OR THAT YOU DID NOT DO IT.

♦ You may mention that you are sorry the person got the wrong impression or that you would like an apology.

Stress the importance of being sincere, not "slick." If the accusation is true, students will need to think about how to make up for what happened—for example, by earning the money to pay for a lost or broken item, giving back a stolen item, or giving a replacement.

SUGGESTED SITUATIONS FOR USING THIS SKILL

1. A teacher has accused you of cheating.

2. Your parent accuses you of breaking something.

3. A friend accuses you of taking something of hers.

4. A neighbor accuses you of breaking his window.

5. Your parent accuses you of having hurt your sibling's feelings with your remark.

6. A friend accuses you of having lied.

7. Your teacher accuses you of being lazy and never finishing your work.

8. Your father accuses you of taking money from his wallet.

EDUCATOR NOTES

Anger reducers (described in chapter 3) such as calming self-talk, deep breathing, and counting are helpful tools to use in this skill.

WEEK 10
Responding Constructively to Failure

**The student does not need a partner for this skill.
Instead, the student explains the situation to the other
two students in the triad.**

STEP 1: ASK YOURSELF, "DID I FAIL?"

♦ Decide if you have failed.

*Explain that there is a difference between failing and not doing quite as well
as you had hoped.*

STEP 2: ASK YOURSELF, "WHY DID I FAIL?"

♦ Think about both the thinking errors and the circumstances that
contributed to your failure.

Ask: "Did you not try as hard as you could have?" "Did you have an over-
confident or self-centered attitude?" "Were you not ready?" "Task too
complicated for you?" "Just unlucky?"

*Encourage students to avoid the Assuming the Worst thinking error and
instead focus on ways to do better next time.*

STEP 3: THINK ABOUT WHAT YOU COULD DO DIFFERENTLY NEXT TIME

*Ask: "Could you practice more?" "Change your attitude or way of thinking?"
"Try harder?" "Ask for help?"*

STEP 4: DECIDE IF YOU WANT TO TRY AGAIN

♦ If you can't try again now, will there be another opportunity later?

STEP 5: IF APPROPRIATE, MAKE A PLAN TO TRY AGAIN

♦ Remember how you can do things differently.

*Encourage students to write down their plans. Stress that "plan" is another
way of saying "think ahead."*

SUGGESTED SITUATIONS FOR USING THIS SKILL

1. You failed a test at school.

2. You failed to complete your chores at home.

3. You failed to get the members of the triad to do the activity you wanted to do.

4. You spent three weeks trying to help your little brother learn how to ride a bicycle, and he still has not learned.

5. You have been working on building a model, but it just does not come out right.

6. You wanted to do at least 30 sit-ups in a row, but you could only do 23.

EDUCATOR NOTES

Responding Constructively to Failure is an important skill for helping students with a Low Self-Image problem and an Assuming the Worst thinking error.

Figure 4.5

Educator's Review and Self-Evaluation Form: Social Skills

Session/Skill _____ **Date** _____

Triad members _____

In General

☐ Yes ☐ No   1. Did triad members follow the ground rules (concerning listening, confidentiality, etc.)?

☐ Yes ☐ No   2. Were all triad members interested and involved? If no, list the names of uninvolved triad members:

_____

_____

_____

☐ Yes ☐ No   3. Did you find some constructive value in every serious comment made by a triad member?

☐ Yes ☐ No   4. Did you maintain a normal voice volume and speak in a respectful rather than threatening or demanding tone?

☐ Yes ☐ No   5. Did you maintain a balance between criticism and approval by using the "sandwich" style of constructive criticism (in which a critical comment is preceded and followed by supportive ones)?

☐ Yes ☐ No   6. Did you appropriately use the ask, don't tell method?

For the Session

☐ Yes ☐ No   1. Did you read and discuss the steps of the social skills on the handout?

☐ Yes ☐ No   2. *(After the first session)* Did you review the previous session's activities?

EQUIP for Educators: Teaching Youth (Grades 5–8) to Think and Act Responsibly © 2005 by A-M. DiBiase, J. C. Gibbs, and G. B. Potter. Champaign, IL: Research Press (800–519–2707; www.researchpress.com).

Educator's Review: Social Skills (continued)

☐ Yes ☐ No   3. Which students tried the skills?

_____

_____

_____

☐ Yes ☐ No   4. *(Discuss the skill.)* Did the designated student members give "coaching" feedback?

☐ Yes ☐ No   5. *(After reading the suggested situations)* Did you encourage triad members to think of a suitable situation from their daily lives in which to try the skill?

☐ Yes ☐ No   6. *(After all triad members tried the skill)* Did triad members receive the Social Skills Practice Sheet?

☐ Yes ☐ No   7. Did you encourage triad members to try the skill outside the session?

CHAPTER
5

EQUIPPING WITH MATURE MORAL JUDGMENT (SOCIAL DECISION MAKING)

At a Columbus, Ohio, middle school for students with behavior problems, 15-year-old Joey was earnest and sincere as he emphatically affirmed the importance of moral values such as helping others, honesty, keeping promises, telling the truth, respecting others' property, and obeying the law. Asked by one of us (Gibbs) why it is so important to obey the law and not steal, Joey exclaimed: "Because, like in a store, you may think no one sees you, but they could have cameras!" His explanations for the importance of other moral values were generally similar: Keeping promises to others is important because if you don't, they might find out and get even; helping others is important in case you need a favor from them later; and so forth.

This chapter provides the procedures and materials for remedying developmental delay in the moral judgment of behaviorally at-risk students. *Delay* is the third and final "D" addressed in this book, the other "D's" being self-serving cognitive *distortions* (chapter 3) and social skill *deficiencies* (chapter 4). At the heart of the three D's are self-centered attitudes (chapter 1), in Aaron Beck's (1999) words the "eye (I) of the storm" of antisocial behavior. Accordingly, at the heart of our psychoeducational curriculum has been the remediation of self-centeredness through the inculcation of social perspective taking skills. For anger management, that means, in part, the teaching of skills for identifying and correcting self-serving thinking errors. For equipping students with social skills, inculcating social perspective taking means, in part, teaching our students to include thinking of others as a step among other steps comprising balanced and constructive social behavior. Remedying moral judgment delays of behaviorally at-risk students is just as important as remedying their cognitive distortions and social skill deficiencies. The 10-week format

Table 5.1 The 10-Week Format for Equipping with Mature Moral Judgment (Social Decision Making)

Week 1	The Martian's Adviser's Problem Situation
Week 2	Jerry's Problem Situation Mateo's Problem Situation
Week 3	Jeff's Problem Situation
Week 4	Angelo's Problem Situation Sabrina's Problem Situation
Week 5	Greg's Problem Situation Lamar's Problem Situation
Week 6	Duane's Problem Situation
Week 7	Joe's Problem Situation
Week 8	Shane's Problem Situation
Week 9	Alfonso's Problem Situation
Week 10	Regina's Problem Situation

for accomplishing this goal, shown in Table 5.1, lists 13 problem situations for students' consideration.

Moral judgment pertains to both the evaluation and the justification of decisions and values pertaining primarily to the right (fairness and justice) and the good (empathy and caring) of human social life (Gibbs, 2003). Joey was emphatic in his positive evaluation of his moral values, but that did not necessarily mean that his moral judgment was mature. If you think Joey's moral reasons or justifications sounded immature for a 15-year-old, you are right. Despite their generally favorable evaluations of moral values (Gregg, Gibbs, & Basinger, 1994), many at-risk students are developmentally delayed in that they do not evidence much grasp of the deeper reasons or bases for those values (although the degree of delay varies according to value area; see Barriga et al., 2001; Gregg et al., 1994; Palmer & Hollin, 1998). How much could Joey be trusted to live up to his moral values in situations where his fear of observers and surveillance cameras is less salient than his egocentric motives and biases? There is something superficial and egocentric, then, about the moral judgment of behaviorally at-risk students.

We interpret at-risk students' superficial and egocentric moral judgment in terms of stage development. In this part of the EQUIP curriculum, the "equipping" moral judgment maturity culminates in a natural direction of development identified by Jean Piaget and Lawrence Kohlberg (see Gibbs, 2003). Our adaptation from Kohlberg's (1984) stage model of moral judgment development is depicted in Table 5.2. During the following discussion, it is important to keep in

Table 5.2   Stages in the Development of Moral Judgment

IMMATURE MORALITIES: STAGES 1 AND 2

Stage 1—Power: "Might Makes Right"
Morality is whatever big or powerful people say that you have to do. If you don't get punished for what you did or no one powerful saw it, whatever you did was okay. It is wrong if you do get punished; the punishment is mainly what makes it wrong.

Stage 2—Deals: "You Scratch My Back, I'll Scratch Yours"
Morality is an exchange of favors ("I did this for you, so you'd better do that for me") or of blows (misunderstanding of the Golden Rule as " Do it to others before they do it to you" or "Pay them back if they've done it to you"). The main reason for not stealing, cheating, and so on is that you could get caught.

MATURE MORALITIES: STAGES 3 AND 4

Stage 3—Mutuality: "Treat Others as You Would Hope They Would Treat You"
In mutual morality, the relationship becomes a value: Trust and mutual caring, although intangible, are real and important. People can really care about other people, can have trust in them, can feel a part of a "we." People try to understand if a friend is acting hostile or selfish.

Stage 4—Systems: "Are You Contributing to Society?"
This morality involves interdependence and cooperation for the sake of society: Society can't make it if people don't respect the rights of others and follow through on commitments. In difficult situations, retaining integrity and self-respect may mean becoming unpopular.

---

mind the stages of moral development. The stages are summarized here. (For more detailed information, see Gibbs, Potter, & Goldstein, 1995, pp. 46–47.)

Moral maturity has to do with mutual caring, respect, or trust—what Piaget (1965/1932) called "ideal reciprocity [or] do as you would be done by" (p. 323)—whether on the scale of interpersonal relationships (Stage 3) or social systems (Stage 4). The immature stages are superficial insofar as they confuse such moral ideals with physical power (Stage 1) or pragmatic deals and advantages or disadvantages (Stage 2). Joey's reasons not to steal, for example, pertained not to interpersonal trust or respect for others or how he would want to be treated (Stage 3) but instead to the prospect of getting caught (Stage 2). And the superficiality of moral judgment developmental delay is egocentric. After all, a superficial reason focuses on something immediately salient like jail or getting caught by a camera—and the immediate desires or impulses of the ego. In the context of moral judgment delay, self-centered attitudes are egocentric biases.

If moral judgment develops through taking and coordinating the perspectives of others, then the developmental delay of many at-risk students should not be surprising. One of our studies (Krevans &

Gibbs, 1996) was consistent with many others in showing that harsh, highly power-assertive, nonreasoning parents have relatively nonempathic, antisocial children. In other words, at-risk students have generally not been taught at home to consider the perspectives of others.

Accordingly, the problem situations and procedures in this chapter provide an enriched, concentrated dose of perspective-taking opportunities to stimulate the delayed students to catch up to an age-appropriate or mature level of moral judgment. The students must justify their decisions in social problem situations set in school, work, home, and other contexts. As others' perspectives are considered in their own right, superficial judgments give way to the construction of more ideal moral understanding. Discussion of the situations is designed to stimulate perspective taking and hence a deeper understanding of the reasons for moral values or decisions such as telling the truth, keeping promises, not stealing or cheating, having honest peer and family relationships, resisting drugs, and preventing a suicide or a school shooting.

The potential of the problem situations to stimulate perspective taking is exploited through their associated probe questions. Some of the probe questions ask students to imagine that *they* are the prospective victims—for example, that a store that is the object of prospective theft is *their* store. Other probe questions ask the students to imagine that the victim of an antisocial act is their sister or another family member—and then to consider whether the act is any less wrong if the victim happens to be a stranger. Still other probe questions ask them to consider how violence (against self or others) affects many others, near and far. We also stimulate the students to remove self-serving impediments to empathy and perspective taking: Planted in some of the probe questions are thinking errors (like blaming the victim) for the students to identify and correct.

Besides the stimulation from the probe questions, challenges to take the perspectives of others are also provided through the format of the class session. The discussion format proceeds through four phases:

1. Introducing the problem situation

2. Cultivating mature morality

3. Remediating developmental delay

4. Consolidating mature morality

Because these phases flow seamlessly from one to the next, they are not easily identifiable. You must continually evaluate what is happening in the group to decide when to move the group to the next phase. A checklist summarizing your facilitative activities is provided in the Educator's Review and Self-Evaluation Form: Mature Moral Judgment (Social Decision Making), given as Figure 5.5 at the end of the chapter. As is the case for the other program components, you should evaluate your work by completing the checklist after the close of each session.

PROCEDURES FOR SOCIAL DECISION MAKING SESSIONS

The procedures for the social decision making sessions resemble, in some ways, those for the anger management or social skill sessions. Just as you prepare for those sessions, for social decision making meetings you will need an easel pad, a marker, and tape to post sheets from the pad. Also, the same ground rules apply to the social decision making sessions. At the outset of each session, you should remind the group of these rules: Never put down or threaten anyone, listen to what others have to say, stay focused on the subject, and so forth (see Table 2.2 for a complete list).

There are also some important procedural differences for the social decision making sessions. Unlike your preparation for the other sessions, for social decision making you will be making charts, as explained and illustrated in the following discussion. These charts are prepared from students' initial decisions on the problem situation handouts.

How you obtain the students' decisions depends on how large your class is (in contrast, class size makes no essential difference in anger management or social skills procedures). In the case of larger classes (more than 12 students), to make the session more manageable, you should divide the class into triads to obtain students' responses. Whether your class is large or small, it is better for the students to answer ahead of time. Distribute copies of the appropriate problem situation handout to your class. Briefly answer any questions about the problem situation, but save elaborations for the introductory phase.

SMALLER CLASSES OR GROUPS

Students in smaller classes or groups (12 or fewer students) consider the problem situation and circle their responses individually. Smaller classes are often composed of behaviorally at-risk students. Even these students will tend to circle positive answers unless they fall prey to their "caring is uncool" peer culture. So do try to make sure your students work independently. (Of course, you can help individual students with any reading problems.) Collect their responses and prepare a chart (preferably ahead of time).

LARGER CLASSES OR GROUPS

Students in larger classes or groups (more than 12 students) read the problem situation as a whole group (you may read it aloud as they follow), then break into triads to discuss it and answer the related questions. One student *records* the triad's answers to each question, while another prepares to *report* the results. The third student, the mediator/negotiator, in each triad *mediates* differences and may report any split answers. When all the triads have made their decisions, the whole class reconvenes, and the triads report. Prepare the chart by recording the triads' decisions.

WHEN SHOULD STUDENTS ANSWER THE PROBLEM SITUATION QUESTIONS?

Whether your class is large or small, we recommend that your students provide their answers prior to the actual social decision making session. Perhaps they can do so in class or at a meeting of the group on the preceding day. The advantage of having students answer the questions before the session is that it helps you prepare for a good discussion. With the students' decisions in hand, you can take time to prepare a chart of students' responses like the ones illustrated in the following pages. You can then study the patterns of decision making among the individual students or triads, looking for prospective strengths and challenges.

- ◆ Who consistently makes the responsible decisions?

- ◆ Which students among those making responsible decisions have relatively mature moral judgment scores (if you did a pretest assessment, as recommended in chapter 2)?

- ◆ Who circled "can't decide" a lot and could go either way?

- ◆ Which students in the group might try to dominate with pragmatic reasons and irresponsible decisions?

If gaining the students' responses ahead of time is not feasible, then you will need to budget time at the beginning of the session itself for this activity.

VALUE OF THE CHARTS

The value of making charts for the social decision making phases can be conveyed with several samples. Figure 5.1 illustrates a hypothetical

Figure 5.1   Responses to the Martian's Adviser's Problem Situation

Name	Planet A	Planet B	Can't Decide
Rachel		X	
Larry	X ⟶	X	
Josie		X	
Mike		X ⟵	X
Nicole	X		
Group Decision		XXXXX	

chart for the first session, pertaining to the Martian's Adviser's Problem Situation (involving the single question, "Which planet would you advise [the Martian] to move to?"). Prepare the chart in the way shown. The students' answers may change during the phases of the social decision making session. The arrows indicate that, after Rachel and Josie explained their decisions (Cultivating Mature Morality, Phase 2), Larry and Mike changed to the positive position (Remediating Moral Developmental Delay, Phase 3). Nicole stayed with her negative stance, but stay tuned: She saw the new group consensus (Consolidating Morality, Phase 4) and may be more amenable to a positive direction in future sessions.

The other problem situations involve multiple questions. A sample chart (with enough rows for the students in a small class) for Jerry's Problem Situation is provided in Figure 5.2. As shown, this chart includes a row to record the majority positions for each of the seven questions about the situation. The teacher or group leader places a question mark after positive majority decisions to each question to indicate that these could become the final group decision on that question. A reproducible copy of this chart is provided as Figure 5.3.

Of course, as with the Martian's Adviser's Problem Situation, some of the students will change their decisions as you help the group cultivate, remediate, and consolidate mature morality.

A reproducible chart for larger groups, designed for recording triads' consensus responses, is given as Figure 5.4. For the purpose of identification, you may give each triad a team number, color, or other designation, or you may have triad members choose their own identifier.

THE FOUR PHASES OF SOCIAL DECISION MAKING

Once you have your social decision making chart, from class activity at the beginning of the session or a prior session, you are ready to lead the group through the four phases of social decision making.

Figure 5.2   Responses to Jerry's Problem Situation

Name	1	2	3	4	5	6	7
					QUESTION NUMBER		
David	party	team	party	party	team	close friend	team
Sara	team	team	team	party	team	close friend	team
Tommy	can't decide	party	team	party	team	close friend	can't decide
Rachel	party	party	party	party	can't decide	close friend	team
Ashley	team	team	team	team	team	can't decide	team
Daniel	party	party	party	party	team	close friend	team
Nicole	party	party	party	party	party	close friend	party
Jonathan	party	party	party	party	party	close friend	team
Brianne	party	party	party	party	party	close friend	party
Group decision	Bob's party?	Bob's party?	Bob's party?	Bob's party?	go with team?	close friend?	go with team?

POSSIBLE GROUP DECISION OUTCOMES

Group decision	Bob's party	Bob's party	Bob's party	Bob's party	go with team?	close friend	go with team?

Figure 5.3   Small-Group Problem Situation Recording Form

Name	QUESTION NUMBER						
	1	2	3	4	5	6	7
Group decision							
	POSSIBLE GROUP DECISION OUTCOMES						
Group decision							

EQUIP for Educators: Teaching Youth (Grades 5–8) to Think and Act Responsibly © 2005 by A-M. DiBiase, J.C. Gibbs, and G.B. Potter. Champaign, IL: Research Press (800–519–2707; www.researchpress.com).

Figure 5.4 Triad Problem Situation Recording Form

Triad	QUESTION NUMBER						
	1	2	3	4	5	6	7
Group decision							

POSSIBLE GROUP DECISION OUTCOMES

Group decision	

EQUIP for Educators: Teaching Youth (Grades 5–8) to Think and Act Responsibly © 2005 by A-M. DiBiase, J.C. Gibbs, and G.B. Potter. Champaign, IL: Research Press (800–519–2707; www.researchpress.com).

Phase 1: Introducing the Problem Situation

To have an effective social decision making session, all students must understand clearly what the problem situation is and how it relates to their lives. You can ask what the problem situation is, why it is a problem, whether problems like this actually happen, and so forth. If there is any question as to whether the group understands the problem situation, we suggest that you have some volunteers from the group role-play the situation. Indeed, we recommend an opening role play as standard practice at the fifth-grade level.

If you have not already done so before class, write down the students' decisions. (The chart shown in Figure 5.4 is designed to guide whole-group discussion of the problem situations.) Remember in the following phases that your role as educator is primarily to facilitate: guide, prompt, and probe as often as needed to develop mature morality, but *do not reduce the discussion to a lecture.*

Phase 2: Cultivating Mature Morality

Once the group understands the problem situation and accepts it as relevant, you can proceed to cultivate a group climate of mature morality—that is, of responsible decisions and mature moral reasons for those decisions. Unless your entire group is consistently or severely delayed, you should have some potential among the students for responsible decisions and reasons. And those students' contributions can be cultivated to promote a positive group culture. A positive peer culture will help render delayed students amenable to positive developmental influence.

Call on the students who have responsible decisions to share their reasons for answering this way. Write those reasons on the easel pad—many are likely to be mature. By calling on the more mature students and writing down their reasons, you are subtly cultivating mature morality. You may even state your agreement with the mature thinkers. If a student wavers and says something like "I know I shouldn't, but I'd probably go ahead and do it," you should reply by relabeling the "should" or "shouldn't" (usually, caring or responsible) action as strong (e.g., "That's true, it would take real guts not to give in to what you feel like doing and instead do what a lot of people might not be strong enough to do—the right thing"). Once you have done what you can to establish a dominant (if not yet unanimous) tone of mature morality, go on to the next phase.

Phase 3: Remediating Moral Developmental Delay

Once a mature moral tone or climate has been cultivated, you can take the problem of developmental delay on directly. After all, the group focus on mature reasons for moral decisions provides a crucial bulwark against the pragmatic influences of students who make negative decisions. These students can seriously undermine the group culture and will do so if allowed. To some extent, you have already started dealing with the developmental delay problem simply by *not* emphasizing the pragmatic among the reasons for the responsible decisions and *not* calling on students who have given negative decisions.

The negative or delayed students cannot be put off forever, however. Although a mature climate may dominate, it is almost certainly not universal in the group. The developmental delay of students who give negative decisions may be moderate or severe; either way, there is need for remediation. You now call on the students who did not have the responsible decisions to share their reasoning. Because "can't decide" may partially reflect responsible thinking, call on the undecided students before calling on those with irresponsible decisions. Record the reasons on the easel pad. Ask mature thinkers to respond to the pragmatic arguments (e.g., "Does David's reason persuade others to change their decision? Why or why not?") You may also have to respectfully challenge these students directly if they are to take the perspectives of others. To challenge self-centered reasons or decisions, you might ask whether such positions are generalizable (e.g., "What would the world be like if everybody did that?" or "Would you still say that if you were the person harmed or wronged in the problem situation?").

Phase 4: Consolidating Mature Morality

Once mature morality has been cultivated and defended, it needs to be consolidated and made as inclusive as possible. The group's mature morality is consolidated—and the group's culture becomes more positive and cohesive—as you seek consensus for positive decisions and mature reasons. As the more pragmatic students, feeling positive pressure, begin to defer to and even embrace mature morality, it is time to invite them to join the majority position. The goal in this final phase is to expand as many of the positive majority positions as possible into group decisions. Refer to the row of the chart next to the bottom, and ask: "Is the group ready to agree [on the decision]? Any objections if someone comes up and crosses out the question mark and circles that as the group's decision?" (Instead of objecting, some may even ask to change their answers to the majority decision. Their answers should be changed accordingly on the chart.) If no one objects, suggest that a volunteer circle the group's official decision. Follow the same procedure for the group's most mature ("top" or "best") reason or reasons, which a volunteer could underline. Don't worry if the group can't reach consensus; a stalemate can be developmentally stimulating, too. In any event, the group should be praised or encouraged at the conclusion of the session. You may even ask the group if they would like to post the sheets showing the group's best decisions and reasons in the classroom.

AFTER THE SESSION

After the session, review the social decision making session and your role as an educator. As noted previously, you can evaluate your effectiveness in terms of the four phases by filling out the Educator's Review and Self-Evaluation Form (Figure 5.5), following the problem situations in this chapter.

THE PROBLEM SITUATIONS

The remainder of this chapter consists of 13 problem situations for use in social decision making sessions. Except for the first problem situation, which has students advising a Martian on where to move (to Planet A or Planet B), the settings for the problems vary from the home to the school. Each situation depicts a student with a problem, typically one created by someone else with a problem (an effective way to induce a nondefensive and more objective discussion of the problems). In addition, each problem situation is accompanied by educator notes, designed to help in processing the material. The pages on which the problem situation and associated questions appear may be reproduced and distributed to students in the course of implementing the program.

The Martian's Adviser's Problem Situation

A man from Mars has decided to move to another planet. He has narrowed his search down to two planets, Planet A and Planet B. Planet A is a violent and dangerous place to live. People just care about themselves and don't care when they hurt others. Planet B is a safer, more peaceful place. People on Planet B do care about others. They still have fun, but they feel bad if they hurt someone. Planet B people try to make the planet a better place.

You are the Martian's adviser. Which planet should you advise him to move to? *(Circle one.)*

Planet A   Planet B   can't decide

EQUIP for Educators: Teaching Youth (Grades 5–8) to Think and Act Responsibly © 2005 by A.-M. DiBiase, J. C. Gibbs, and G. B. Potter. Champaign, IL: Research Press (800–519–2707; www.researchpress.com).

EDUCATOR NOTES
The Martian's Adviser's Problem Situation

KEY VALUE: AFFILIATION

The Martian's Adviser's Problem Situation defines the opening sessions. Whereas later situations stimulate the development of moral judgment, this situation is designed mainly to facilitate the discovery of common values, and thereby to foster a cohesive, prosocial group culture.

It is important to emphasize that every student would like, not only for the Martian but for himself or herself, a world that is positive (safer, more caring, more prosocial, and so on). If some students have chosen and argued for the negative planet, the majority should be challenged to refute them. The group thereby begins to cohere in the endorsement of these positive values.

Some reasons for choosing Planet B come from the problem situation context:

◆ There is not as much violence.

◆ It is more peaceful.

◆ People get along without fighting; people want to help one another.

◆ People have fun without hurting others.

◆ People work to make things better.

Other reasons include the following:

◆ You can live longer.

◆ There's less crime.

◆ There's better listening or communication.

◆ People are more trustworthy.

◆ They try to control their anger.

◆ People apologize.

◆ Parents spend more time with their kids.

A few students may choose Planet A for the following reasons:

◆ You could do whatever you want, whenever you want it.

◆ People would not be sticking their nose in your business.

The students should be challenged to make the group a Planet B. The following specific probe questions may be helpful:

1. What is the basic thinking error, the basic problem, on Planet A?

The answer, Self-Centered, should be fairly easy to elicit.

2. *(To those favoring Planet A because no one bothers you or if the group needs assistance)* What if someone you did care about—say a parent or brother or sister or close friend—was going to commit suicide? Would you let the person do it and not "bother" him or her? That's what Planet A would be like.

Prompt the group to consider such a world. Typically, Planet A respondents will acquiesce so that the Planet B choice becomes unanimous. Use relabeling to make sure that caring is not stigmatized as weak.

3. Where are the truly strong people? On Planet A or on Planet B?

This question helps apply the "planet" to the group.

4. What kind of group do you want this group to be—Planet A or Planet B, negative or positive? It's up to you. If Planet B is what you want for this group, have you been living up to it? Planet B won't happen unless everyone practices what he or she preaches to make it happen. *(Relabeling again)* But it's not easy. It takes courage; it takes strength.

Most students will select the positive Planet B. Sometimes this problem situation will stimulate soul-searching.

5. Who has had a friend or acquaintance die a violent death?

Among at-risk students in an urban environment, usually at least a few students will raise their hands or speak up.

6. What do people say about the person—what kind of difference did he or she make?

7. What kind of difference will people say you made?

Explain: "It's not too early to start thinking about your life—how you're living it, what kind of difference you want to make. Some of your friends may have said they value a Planet B, but their behavior made things more like Planet A."

8. What about you?

* * *

During the discussion illustrated in Figure 5.1, mature morality was (a) cultivated (a positive decision was supported by mature reasons),

(b) remediated (Larry's and Mike's answers changed to a positive decision with mature reasons), and (c) consolidated (the group arrived at a positive decision, mature reasoning).

After this session, "Planet A" and "Planet B" become part of the group vocabulary:

◆ A collection of individual self-centered and selfish attitudes characterized by mistrust and disruption is "Planet A."

◆ A climate of mutual caring and trust characterized by well-equipped help for students is "Planet B."

These terms provide "handles" for contrasting group atmospheres. Such handles make it easier for youths who are otherwise concrete thinkers to bring to mind group-level weaknesses and ideals. In subsequent sessions, instead of simply asking how the group thinks things have been going, you may ask whether the group has slipped back toward Planet A or continued to progress toward Planet B.

Jerry's Problem Situation

Jerry had just moved to a new school and was feeling pretty lonely until one day a guy named Bob came up and introduced himself. "Hi, Jerry. My name is Bob. I heard one of the teachers say you are new here. If you are not doing anything after school today, how about coming over to play some basketball?" Pretty soon, Jerry and Bob were good friends.

One day when Jerry was shooting baskets by himself, the basketball coach saw him and invited him to try out for the team. Jerry made the team, and every day after school he would practice with the rest of the team. After practice, Jerry and his teammates would always hang out together. On weekends sometimes they would go over to each other's house.

As Jerry spends more time with the team, he sees less and less of Bruno, his old friend. One day, Jerry gets a call from Bob. "Say, I was wondering," says Bob, "if you are not too busy on Thursday, my family is having a little birthday party for me." Jerry tells Bob he'll try to come to the party. But during practice on Thursday, everyone tells Jerry about the great place they are all going to after practice.

What should Jerry say or do?

1. Should Jerry go with the team? *(Circle one.)*

   go with team   go to Bob's party   can't decide

2. What if Jerry calls Bruno from school and says he is sorry, but something has come up and he can't come over after all? *(Circle one.)*

   go with team   go to Bob's party   can't decide

3. What if Jerry considers that his teammates may be upset if Jerry doesn't come—that they may start to think Jerry's not such a good friend? Then would it be all right for Jerry to go with the team? *(Circle one.)*

   go with team   go to Bob's party   can't decide

4. What if Jerry thinks that, after all, Bruno came along and helped Jerry when Jerry was lonely. Then should Jerry go with the team? *(Circle one.)*

   go with team   go to Bob's party   can't decide

EQUIP for Educators: Teaching Youth (Grades 5–8) to Think and Act Responsibly © 2005 by A-M. DiBiase, J. C. Gibbs, and G. B. Potter. Champaign, IL: Research Press (800–519–2707; www.researchpress.com).

Jerry's Problem Situation (continued)

5. Let's change the situation a bit: Let's say that before Bob asks Jerry to come over, the teammates ask if Jerry will be coming along on Thursday. Jerry says he thinks so. Then Bob asks Jerry. Then what should Jerry do? *(Circle one.)*

   go with team   go to Bob's party   can't decide

6. Which is more important: to have one close friend or to have a group of regular friends? *(Circle one.)*

   go with team   go to Bob's party   can't decide

7. Let's change the situation a different way: What if Jerry and Bob are not good friends but instead are just acquaintances? Then should Jerry go with the team? *(Circle one.)*

   go with team   go to Bob's party   can't decide

EDUCATOR NOTES
Jerry's Problem Situation

KEY VALUES: RELATIONSHIP AND RESPECT

Discussion of Jerry's Problem Situation typically promotes a more profound or mature understanding of friendship. Some more severely delayed students (those students who consistently reason at a level no higher than moral judgment Stage 2) may actually become stimulated to construct Stage 3 moral judgment. For others who already understand and use Stage 3 to some extent, mature reasoning may become more prominent.

Discussion of the value of close friendships seems to promote social cohesion. In this way, Jerry's Problem Situation continues the cultivation of the group that began with the discussion of the Martian's Adviser's Problem Situation.

Student discussion is key regarding Question 6; often the choice of "one close friend" is unanimous. Reasons for this choice may include the suggestions that "you can tell a close friend anything" and "a close friend can be trusted not to take advantage of you." Especially for this question, Jerry's Problem Situation permits the cultivation and consolidation of mature morality.

Once a positive peer atmosphere is achieved through listening and discussion of the reasons for the majority position, attention can turn to the dissenting students. The few members advocating that Jerry go with the team tend to be unabashed hedonists (i.e., in zealous pursuit of pleasure). They may say, for example, "Jerry would have more fun with the team." They may also try to minimize the harm done to Bob: "Bob won't even notice Jerry didn't come."

The main question on which the majority might choose "go with the team" is Question 7, which changes the nature of the relationship between Jerry and Bob from friendship to acquaintance. To a lesser extent, the majority may also choose "go with the team" for Question 5, which has Jerry making the first commitment to the team rather than to Bob. Those students for whom the prior commitment to Bob was the important factor will tend to switch the "team" response on Question 5.

Mateo's Problem Situation

Mateo has been going out with a girl named Martina for about two months. It used to be a lot of fun to be with her, but lately it's been a little boring. There are some other girls Mateo would like to go out with now. Mateo sees Martina coming down the school hallway.

What should Mateo say or do?

1. Should Mateo avoid the subject with Martina so Martina's feelings are not hurt? *(Circle one.)*

   should avoid subject   should bring it up   can't decide

2. Should Mateo make up an excuse, like being too busy to see Martina, as a way of breaking up? *(Circle one.)*

   excuse   no excuse   can't decide

3. Should Mateo simply start seeing other girls so that Martina will get the message? *(Circle one.)*

   yes   no   can't decide

4. How should Mateo respond to Martina's feelings?

   _____

   _____

   _____

5. Let's go back to the original situation. This is what happens: Mateo does break up with Martina—he lets her know how he feels and starts dating another girl. Martina feels hurt and jealous and thinks about getting even somehow. Should Martina get even? *(Circle one.)*

   yes, should get even   no, shouldn't get even   can't decide

6. What if the tables were turned, and Martina did that to Mateo? Should Mateo get even? *(Circle one.)*

   yes, should get even   no, shouldn't get even   can't decide

EQUIP for Educators: Teaching Youth (Grades 5–8) to Think and Act Responsibly © 2005 by A-M. DiBiase, J.C. Gibbs, and G.B. Potter. Champaign, IL: Research Press (800–519–2707; www.researchpress.com).

EDUCATOR NOTES
Mateo's Problem Situation

KEY VALUES: RELATIONSHIP AND RESPECT

Mateo's Problem Situation continues the theme of mature, caring relationships but focuses on the problem of how to respect one another in ending a dating relationship. Try to cultivate a mature discussion (e.g., one student suggested that Mateo could say, "I think we should see other people. What do you think?") before tackling the questions on vengeance.

It is sometimes helpful to ask the students exactly what is meant by "getting even." Responses might range from "showing off" (to Martina) with a new girlfriend to spreading rumors about one another to physical assault. These types of responses, once stated for group consideration, will often be branded as immature or destructive by the majority.

If the group is still developing, you may need to model relabeling—that is, comment on the strength and courage it takes not to "give in to immature desires to get even."

The degree of positive content in this session may be surprising and should be encouraged. It is important to comment on the great potential the group has shown for becoming a positive or "Planet B" group. Using the "Planet" vocabulary in relabeling, emphasize that a "Planet A" place is full of weak people who give in to their selfishness and immaturity, and a strong group is one in which members care about one another's feelings.

Bear in mind, however, that the students expressing more negative sentiments may be speaking more candidly; their words may be consistent with the actual behavior of the majority. After all, consider how common "payback" or vengeance is in the daily life of a school. Similarly, in social skills exercises, the initial absence of caring about another's feelings is often striking. Clearly, the students' challenge is to consolidate mature morality not only in terms of responsible thoughts or words but also responsible actions.

Jeff's Problem Situation

Jeff and Darrell are friends. Jeff, whose birthday is coming up, has mentioned to Darrell how great it would be to have a CD player to listen to music while doing his homework. Darrell steals a CD player from someone's open locker. Jeff is appreciative, not realizing it was stolen.

The next day, Jeff sees Steve, another friend. Jeff knows Steve has a CD player and lots of CDs. Jeff mentions that he got a CD player for a birthday present and asks Steve to come over and trade CDs. "Sure," Steve says with a sigh.

"You look down, Steve. What's wrong?" Jeff asks.

"Oh, I was ripped off," Steve says.

"Oh, boy. What did they get?" Jeff asks.

"My CD player," Steve says. Steve starts describing the stolen CD player.

Later, Jeff starts thinking about how odd it is that Steve's CD player was stolen just at the time Darrell gave him one. Jeff gets suspicious and calls Darrell. Sure enough, Darrell confesses that he stole it, and the CD player he stole turns out to be Steve's.

It's time for Steve to arrive at Darrell's. Steve will probably recognize the CD player as his. Steve is at the door, ringing the doorbell. **What should Jeff—the one who got the stolen present from Darrell—do or say?**

1. Should Jeff tell Steve that Darrell took Steve's CD player? *(Circle one.)*

    should tell   shouldn't tell   can't decide

2. How good a friend is Darrell? Would Jeff be able to trust Darrell not to steal from him? *(Circle one.)*

    yes, could trust   no, couldn't trust   can't decide

3. Darrell stole the CD player for a good cause (Jeff's birthday). Does that make it all right for Darrell to steal it? *(Circle one.)*

    yes, all right   no, not all right   can't decide

4. What if Darrell didn't steal the CD player from Steve's locker? What if instead Darrell stole the CD player from a stranger's locker? Then would it be all right for Darrell to steal it for Jeff's birthday? *(Circle one.)*

    yes, all right   no, not all right   can't decide

EQUIP for Educators: Teaching Youth (Grades 5–8) to Think and Act Responsibly © 2005 by A-M. DiBiase, J.C. Gibbs, and G.B. Potter. Champaign, IL: Research Press (800–519–2707; www.researchpress.com).

EDUCATOR NOTES
Jeff's Problem Situation

KEY VALUES: HONESTY AND RESPECT FOR PROPERTY

Jeff's Problem Situation continues the theme of positive caring and friendship embodied in the Martian's Adviser's, Jerry's, and Mateo's situations, but it focuses on the importance of trust in a friendship. How trustworthy is a friend who has a stealing problem? Should you tell on a friend who has stolen in order to give you a gift? Or is stealing all right if it's for a friend?

Insofar as this problem situation addresses the value not only of affiliation but also of property, it serves as an excellent transition to many of the problem situations that follow.

Through most of the questions, you should be able to cultivate a sense of the importance of trust and even consolidate mature morality for the discussion in these terms. The most controversial question is whether Jeff should tell on Darrell (Question 1). Some students might favor telling, emphasizing that Darrell took a risk and now has to face up to what he did; if Jeff doesn't tell, he becomes involved in Darrell's stealing, and Darrell is also a friend (after all, he stole because he wanted to do something nice for Jeff), and you should never rat on a friend.

Students acknowledge the importance of disciplining Darrell but caution against getting Steve involved—they might offer lurid descriptions, in fact, of what Steve would do to Darrell. It might be difficult to persuade the students to reach a unanimous decision on Question 1.

Students might also argue that it would have been all right for Darrell to steal a CD player for Jeff's birthday if only it had not belonged to one of Jeff's friends. If no one in the group can be prompted to challenge this thinking, you may need to (e.g., "So if you were the stranger, is it OK if someone stole your CD player?").

Angelo's Problem Situation

Angelo is walking along a side street with his friend Ramon. Noticing a purse in the backseat of a parked car, Ramon stops and tries the car door. Ramon says, excitedly, "Look! The car's unlocked, and there's a purse in the backseat. Let's grab it!"

What should Angelo say or do?

1. Should Angelo try to persuade Ramon not to steal the purse? *(Circle one.)*

   should persuade   should let steal   can't decide

2. What if Ramon says to Angelo that the car is unlocked and that anyone that careless deserves to get ripped off. Then should Angelo try to persuade Ramon not to steal the purse? *(Circle one.)*

   should persuade   should let steal   can't decide

3. What if Ramon says to Angelo that the car owner can probably get insurance money to cover things taken from the car? *(Circle one.)*

   should persuade   should let steal   can't decide

4. What if Ramon tells Angelo that stealing from cars is no big deal, that plenty of his friends do it all the time? Then what should Angelo do? *(Circle one.)*

   should persuade   should let steal   can't decide

5. Let's say the car is *your* car. Then should Angelo try to persuade Ramon not to steal the purse? *(Circle one.)*

   should persuade   should let steal   can't decide

6. In general, how important is it for people not to take things that belong to others? *(Circle one.)*

   very important   important   not important

EQUIP for Educators: Teaching Youth (Grades 5–8) to Think and Act Responsibly © 2005 by A-M. DiBiase, J.C. Gibbs, and G.B. Potter. Champaign, IL: Research Press (800–519–2707; www.researchpress.com).

EDUCATOR NOTES
Angelo's Problem Situation

KEY VALUES: HONESTY AND RESPECT FOR PROPERTY

Like Jeff in the preceding problem situation, Angelo must contend with a friend who has a stealing problem. The majority position should be that Angelo should try to persuade Ramon not to steal the purse (Questions 1 through 6) and that it is very important not to steal.

Mature reasons appeal to the danger and harm to innocent people (including the car owner), to the way one would feel if it was a parent's purse, and to the loss of order if everyone stole. Students should notice the Blaming Others error in laying blame on the victim (Question 2). In general, this problem situation offers fairly good prospects for cultivating and consolidating mature morality, although you might hear pragmatic and mature reasons in support of the majority positions.

Thinking errors are plentiful in the pragmatic reasoning. For example, some students might say, "Everyone steals anyway"; "You'd teach the person a good lesson—not to be so careless"; and "The car owner is a dummy, fool, or jerk for leaving the keys" (Minimizing/ Mislabeling). If triad members do not catch and correct these thinking errors, the teacher should intervene to do so. Angelo's Problem Situation is an especially good situation for discussing the gap between moral judgment and moral action. Many students who proffer superbly mature and compelling reasons for trying to persuade Ramon not to steal the purse might disclose at some point in the discussion that they would probably join Ramon: "I know I shouldn't, but I probably would." It is important to listen actively but also relabel: "That's right. This is a tough situation to keep your head in. It does take a lot of guts to say no and do the right thing."

You can also remind the students of the skill Dealing Constructively with Negative Peer Pressure, which they learned in the social skills program component (see chapter 4, Week 3). Preview that skill if your group has not learned it yet.

Sabrina's Problem Situation

Sabrina works after school as a cashier in a small grocery store. The store isn't too busy. Rico, a younger friend of Sabrina's at school, comes over to her cash register and says, "Hey, let me take this pack of cigarettes, okay? The manager is at the back of the store—he'll never know." Rico is Sabrina's friend, but Sabrina knows the manager trusts her.

What should Sabrina say or do?

1. Should Sabrina refuse Rico, or should Sabrina say yes to Rico's suggestion? *(Circle one.)*

   should refuse   should say yes   can't decide

2. Was it right for Rico to put Sabrina on the spot with his request? *(Circle one.)*

   yes, right   no, not right   can't decide

3. What if Sabrina feels that other employees at the store do this for their friends? Then what should Sabrina do? *(Circle one.)*

   should refuse   should say yes   can't decide

4. What if Sabrina remembers that the manager is trusting her? Then what should Sabrina do? *(Circle one.)*

   should refuse   should say yes   can't decide

5. What if you are the owner of the grocery store where Sabrina is working? Then what should Sabrina do? *(Circle one.)*

   should refuse   should say yes   can't decide

6. How important is it to be honest at a store where you work? *(Circle one.)*

   very important   important   not important

EQUIP for Educators: Teaching Youth (Grades 5–8) to Think and Act Responsibly © 2005 by A-M. DiBiase, J.C. Gibbs, and G.B. Potter. Champaign, IL: Research Press (800–519–2707; www.researchpress.com).

EDUCATOR NOTES
Sabrina's Problem Situation

KEY VALUES: HONESTY AND RESPECT FOR PROPERTY

Like Jeff and Angelo before her, Sabrina must deal with an awkward situation created by a friend with a stealing problem. And, like Jeff and Angelo, Sabrina may get into serious difficulties if she does not make the right decision.

Sabrina's Problem Situation is also very similar to Angelo's: In each situation, the protagonist is experiencing pressure from a "friend" to join in something dishonest—stealing a purse in Alfonso's case; stealing from a store in Sabrina's.

This situation may provoke a vigorous discussion. Many students may argue for saying yes to Rico, suggesting that Sabrina can get away with it, that maybe she likes Rico, that he's a friend who has done favors for her, that she needs to pay him back, that she needs to get him off her back, that maybe then he'll help her out sometime, or that he'll get even with her if she doesn't help him.

Some students may suggest that Sabrina could pay out of her own pocket to make up the difference so that the store isn't hurt. In the ideal group discussion, students will effectively rebut these assertions without intervention from you—for example, "What kind of a friend would put you on the spot like that?" or "Will this really be the end of it, or will Rico only try this again, tell his friends, and get more and more demanding?"

If the more mature students effectively remediate their peers' immature thinking, then you not only cultivate but also consolidate mature morality.

Greg's Problem Situation

One day, Greg's older brother, Josh, tells him a secret: Josh is selling drugs. Greg and Josh both know that the kind of drug Josh is selling is highly addictive and causes lung and brain damage. It can even kill people. Josh says he is only doing it to help out with the family's money problems and asks Greg not to tell anyone.

What should Greg say or do?

1. Should Greg promise to keep quiet and not tell on his brother? *(Circle one.)*

   should keep quiet   should tell   can't decide

2. What if Josh tells Greg that selling drugs is no big deal—that plenty of Josh's friends do it all the time? Then what should Greg do? *(Circle one.)*

   keep quiet   tell   can't decide

3. What if Greg finds out that Josh is selling the drug to 10-year-olds outside a school? Then what should Greg do? *(Circle one.)*

   keep quiet   tell   can't decide

4. What if Josh himself won't be harmed by the drug—he tells Greg he knows how addictive and harmful the stuff is and never touches it? Then what should Greg do? *(Circle one.)*

   keep quiet   tell   can't decide

5. What if Greg finds out that Josh isn't using any of the money at all to help out the family, but is spending it on things for himself instead? Then what should Greg do? *(Circle one.)*

   keep quiet   tell   can't decide

6. Is it right to tell on someone? *(Circle one.)*

   sometimes right   never right   can't decide

7. Who is to blame in this situation? *(Circle one.)*

   Greg (younger brother)   Josh (drug dealer)   can't decide

8. How important is it for judges to send drug dealers to jail? *(Circle one.)*

   very important   important   can't decide

EQUIP for Educators: Teaching Youth (Grades 5–8) to Think and Act Responsibly © 2005 by A-M. DiBiase, J.C. Gibbs, and G.B. Potter. Champaign, IL: Research Press (800–519–2707; www.researchpress.com).

EDUCATOR NOTES
Greg's Problem Situation

KEY VALUES: QUALITY OF LIFE, LIFE

In Greg's Problem Situation, the stakes are raised with respect to the issue of dealing with an irresponsible person. Instead of a CD player or purse (Jeff's or Angelo's Problem Situation), or an off-limits item like cigarettes (Sabrina's Problem Situation), the drugs Greg's brother sells can seriously harm those who buy them. So, with this problem situation, it should be easier to cultivate and consolidate mature morality.

Greg's Problem Situation is controversial. Some antisocial youths might be dealing in drugs themselves and identify with Josh. Students who advocate not telling might assert that what Josh does is none of Greg's business, that Greg should let Josh learn a lesson, that Josh could be making a lot of money and not be in danger at all, that someone else will sell the stuff and make money if Josh doesn't, that Josh isn't forcing anyone to buy anything, and that Greg could get killed if he tells on Josh.

Alert majority-position students may rebut these points: It is Greg's business if the family is endangered, the "lesson" is too expensive if it's a brother's death, Josh is forcing the drug on 10-year olds (Question 3) because "they don't know what they are doing," and "Josh is kidding himself if he thinks he is not in any danger—you can't sell drugs and not be in danger."

Maturing students may also point out the hypocrisy involved in Josh's not taking the drug himself (Question 4): "He won't hurt himself, but he will make money off hurting others—dealing death to others." Some controversy will probably also arise concerning the importance of sending drug dealers to jail (Question 8). Some students may argue for merely "important" or even "not important" on the grounds that sending drug dealers to jail is "useless" or "hopeless" because you can't send enough of them to make a dent in the problem.

Again, alert majority-position students may invoke the thinking error vocabulary to brand this an Assuming the Worst mistake. They may point out that this is exactly how the drug world wants you to think and that avoiding this mistake means doing what you can rather than doing nothing.

Lamar's Problem Situation

Just after Lamar arrived at an institution for boys, he tried to escape. As a result, he was given extra time. It took Lamar nearly four months to earn the trust of the staff again. He now thinks it is stupid to try to leave. However, Bruno, a friend of Lamar's, tells Lamar he is planning to escape that night. "I've got it all figured out," Bruno says. "I'll hit the youth leader on the head with a pipe and take his keys." Bruno asks Lamar to come along. Lamar tries to talk Bruno out of it, but Bruno won't listen.

What should Lamar say or do?

1. Should Lamar tell the staff about Bruno's plan to escape? *(Circle one.)*

    tell   keep quiet   can't decide

2. What if Bruno is a pretty violent type of guy and Lamar thinks that Bruno might seriously injure, maybe even kill, the youth leader? Then what should Lamar do? *(Circle one.)*

    tell   keep quiet   can't decide

3. What if the youth leader is mean, and everyone hates him? Then what should Lamar do? *(Circle one.)*

    tell   keep quiet   can't decide

4. Is it any of Lamar's business what Bruno does? *(Circle one.)*

    can be Lamar's   is none of Lamar's   can't decide
    business   business

5. Is it ever any of Lamar's business what Bruno does? *(Circle one.)*

    yes, sometimes   no, never   can't decide

6. Let's change the situation a bit: Let's say the youth leader is Lamar's uncle. Then what should Lamar do? *(Circle one.)*

    tell   keep quiet   can't decide

7. Let's change the situation a different way: Let's say Bruno is Lamar's brother. Then what should Lamar do? *(Circle one.)*

    tell   keep quiet   can't decide

8. Which is the most important? *(Circle one.)*

    not telling on   not letting other   minding your own
    your friend   people get hurt   business

EQUIP for Educators: Teaching Youth (Grades 5–8) to Think and Act Responsibly © 2005 by A-M. DiBiase, J.C. Gibbs, and G.B. Potter. Champaign, IL: Research Press (800–519–2707; www.researchpress.com).

Lamar's Problem Situation

This problem situation is intended for more seriously at-risk students.

KEY VALUES: QUALITY OF LIFE, LIFE

Again, the group faces the problem of dealing with a troublesome friend. Lamar must deal with a friend whose actions may be life threatening. Although Lamar's friend is not dealing in deadly drugs, he is planning a crime in which someone could get killed.

It should be possible to cultivate and consolidate mature morality, especially for Questions 5 (when the youth leader is Lamar's uncle) and 7 (when Bruno is Lamar's brother).

Some students may argue that what Bruno does is none of Lamar's business and so Lamar shouldn't get involved. After all, Bruno would be killing someone everyone hates (Question 3). Alert majority-group members may counter that Bruno has made it Lamar's business by telling Lamar of his plans and that the youth leader does not deserve to get killed.

Duane's Problem Situation

Duane's friend Max does some drug dealing. Once in a while Max even gives Duane some for free. Now Max says to Duane, "Listen, I've got to deliver some stuff on the south side, but I can't do it myself. How about it? Will you take the stuff down there for me in your car? I'll give you some new stuff to try plus $50 besides for just a half an hour's bike ride. Will you help me out?"

What should Duane say or do?

1. Should Duane agree to deliver the drugs for Max? *(Circle one.)*

   yes, should deliver   no, shouldn't deliver can't decide

2. What if Duane knows that the drugs Max wants him to deliver are laced with poison? Should he agree to deliver them? *(Circle one.)*

   yes, should deliver   no, shouldn't deliver can't decide

3. What if Duane knows that his sister, who lives on the south side, might take some of the laced stuff? Then should he agree to deliver it? *(Circle one.)*

   yes, should deliver   no, shouldn't deliver can't decide

4. Should Duane be taking the free stuff from Max? *(Circle one.)*

   yes, should take it   no, shouldn't take it can't decide

5. What if Max says that doing drugs is no big deal, that plenty of his friends use drugs all the time? Then should Duane be taking the free drugs? *(Circle one.)*

   yes   no   can't decide

6. Let's say that Duane does make the drug delivery. Since Duane is just helping out Max, he doesn't feel he is doing anything wrong. Should Duane feel he is doing something wrong? *(Circle one.)*

   yes, wrong   no, not wrong   can't decide

7. How important is it to stay away from drugs? *(Circle one.)*

   very important   important   can't decide

EQUIP for Educators: Teaching Youth (Grades 5–8) to Think and Act Responsibly © 2005 by A-M. DiBiase, J. C. Gibbs, and G. B. Potter. Champaign, IL: Research Press (800–519–2707; www.researchpress.com).

EDUCATOR NOTES
Duane's Problem Situation

Key Value: Quality of Life

Like the protagonists in previous problem situations, Duane finds himself placed in an awkward position by an irresponsible friend. Once again, a protagonist must cope with negative peer pressure. Should Duane help out his drug-trafficking friend by making a drug delivery?

The majority position tends to be responsible, especially for Questions 2 (the drugs laced with poison) and 3 (Duane's sister may get the drugs). Accordingly, for these questions it should be possible to cultivate and consolidate mature morality.

Nonetheless, Duane's Problem Situation is often controversial. A few students—and sometimes even a majority— might argue that Duane should make the drug delivery. Their reasoning is purely pragmatic: "Duane's been doing drugs anyway"; "Max's offering a good deal—Duane can make some money"; "This could lead to bigger opportunities"; "If Duane doesn't do it, someone else will anyway"; "No one's forcing anyone to take anything"; "It's their fault if they get hurt"; and "You've got to take care of yourself before you worry about anyone else." You may have to intervene to correct these errors. If a student cannot identify the Minimizing/Mislabeling and Assuming the Worst errors, then the leader must assert that in fact most people do think ahead and think of others and most people won't sell people things that will kill them just so they can make money off them: That's why most people don't commit crimes and are not locked up.

Relabeling will help: "It's certainly possible to think before you act and make the responsible choice—although no one said it was easy; it does take a lot of personal strength." Encouragement is also in order: "I have seen you in action—I know this can be a Planet B group, and with the group's help, each of you can become strong enough to think before you hurt people again. The bottom line is what kind of life each of you is going to decide to live, what kind of difference you want to make in your life: one for the better, or one for the worse."

As with Angelo's Problem Situation, it may be helpful to apply the social skill Dealing Constructively with Negative Peer Pressure (see chapter 4, Week 3). In this connection, the group leader should emphasize that Duane does have a choice: "People do not choose to catch a cold from a friend, but they do make a choice when they accept drugs offered by a friend."

Joe's Problem Situation

Joe and Jamal are students at a middle school. They get along well and have become good friends. Jamal has confided that he has been depressed and angry lately, especially at the school principal, and that he has managed to get hold of his father's gun. Joe sees the gun hidden in Jamal's locker. Jamal has asked Joe not to say anything, but Joe is concerned that Jamal may shoot himself or others.

What should Joe say or do?

1. Should Joe cover for Jamal and not say anything about the gun? *(Circle one.)*

   cover for Jamal tell the principal can't decide

2. What if Jamal has told Joe that he has made plans to shoot himself or others? Then what should Joe do? *(Circle one.)*

   cover for Jamal tell the principal can't decide

3. Would Jamal feel that Joe cared about him if Joe told? *(Circle one.)*

   yes, would feel no, would not feel can't decide
   Joe cared   Joe cared

4. How important is it for a school to have rules against smuggling weapons into school? *(Circle one.)*

   very important important can't decide

5. How important is it to live even when you do not want to? *(Circle one.)*

   very important important can't decide

6. Who else might be affected (in addition to Jamal himself) if Jamal were to commit suicide?

   _____

   _____

   _____

EQUIP for Educators: Teaching Youth (Grades 5–8) to Think and Act Responsibly © 2005 by A-M. DiBiase, J.C. Gibbs, and G.B. Potter. Champaign, IL: Research Press (800–519–2707; www.researchpress.com).

EDUCATOR NOTES
Joe's Problem Situation

KEY VALUE: LIFE

How to deal with an irresponsible friend is again the problem. With Joe's Problem Situation, however, the life threatened by the friend's activity is not someone else's, as in Greg's Problem Situation, but instead the friend's own life.

Because the majority positions tend to be responsible (tell the principal, etc.), you should be able to cultivate and consolidate mature morality. Some students may advocate covering for Jamal on the grounds that Joe should mind his own business and not get involved.

Others may assert that living even when you don't want to (Question 5) is not important because "It's your life—you can do whatever you want with it." Because it concerns life and death, Joe's Problem Situation invites consideration of existential/spiritual concerns, especially for older students.

Shane's Problem Situation

Shane and his friend John are shopping in a music store. Shane has driven them to the store. John picks up a CD he really likes and slips it into his backpack. With a little sign to Shane to follow, John then walks out of the store. But Shane doesn't see John. Moments later, the security officer and the store owner come up to Shane. The store owner says to the officer, "That's one of the boys who were stealing CDs!" The security officer checks Shane's backpack but doesn't find a CD. "Okay, you're off the hook, but what's the name of the guy who was with you?" the officer asks Shane. "I'm almost broke because of shoplifting," the owner says. "I can't let him get away with it."

What should Shane say or do?

1. Should Shane keep quiet and refuse to tell the security officer John's name? *(Circle one.)*

   keep quiet   tell   can't decide

2. From the store owner's point of view, what should Shane do? *(Circle one.)*

   keep quiet   tell   can't decide

3. What if the store owner is a nice guy who sometimes lets kids buy CDs even if they don't have quite enough money? Then what should Shane do? *(Circle one.)*

   keep quiet   tell   can't decide

4. What if the store owner is Shane's father? Then what should Shane do? *(Circle one.)*

   keep quiet   tell   can't decide

5. Is it ever right to tell on someone? *(Circle one.)*

   yes, sometimes   no, never   can't decide

6. Who's to blame in this situation? *(Circle one.)*

   Shane   John   store owner   can't decide

7. How important is it not to shoplift? *(Circle one.)*

   very important important   not important can't decide

8. How important is it for store owners to prosecute shoplifters? *(Circle one.)*

   very important   important   not important   can't decide

EQUIP for Educators: Teaching Youth (Grades 5–8) to Think and Act Responsibly © 2005 by A-M. DiBiase, J.C. Gibbs, and G.B. Potter. Champaign, IL: Research Press (800–519–2707; www.researchpress.com).

EDUCATOR NOTES
Shane's Problem Situation

KEY VALUES: HONESTY AND RESPECT FOR PROPERTY

With Shane's Problem Situation, the "telling on an irresponsible friend" issue reverts from life (e.g., Joe's Problem Situation) to property (e.g., Sabrina's Problem Situation). You should be able to cultivate and consolidate mature morality, especially on Questions 3 (What if the store owner is nice to kids?) and 4 (What if the store owner is Sam's father?). Consensus might not be possible on all questions.

Dissenters may argue against "ratting on your friend" and suggest that Shane can best stay out of trouble by keeping quiet: "They can't get him—he doesn't have to say anything." These students may also attribute blame to the store owner (Question 6) on the grounds that the owner should have had customers check things like backpacks before they came in. Alert students will point out the Blaming Others error in such an attribution.

Alfonso's Problem Situation

Alfonso is in school taking a math test. Suddenly, the teacher says, "I'm going to leave the room for a few minutes. You are on your honor not to cheat." After the teacher has gone, Doug, Alfonso's friend, whispers to him, "Let me see your answers, Alfonso."

What should Alfonso say or do?

1. Should Alfonso let Doug copy his answers? *(Circle one.)*

   yes, let cheat   no, don't let cheat   can't decide

2. What if Doug whispers that cheating is no big deal, that he knows plenty of guys who cheat all the time? Then should Alfonso let Doug cheat? *(Circle one.)*

   yes, let cheat   no, don't let cheat   can't decide

3. What if Alfonso knows that Doug is flunking because he doesn't study? Then should Alfonso let Doug cheat? *(Circle one.)*

   yes, let cheat   no, don't let cheat   can't decide

4. What if you were the teacher? Would you want Alfonso to let Doug cheat? *(Circle one.)*

   yes, let cheat   no, don't let cheat   can't decide

5. Is it possible to have a really close, trusting friendship with someone who has a cheating or lying problem? *(Circle one.)*

   yes, possible   no, not possible   can't decide

6. Let's change the situation a little. What if Alfonso hardly knows Doug? Then should Alfonso let Doug cheat? *(Circle one.)*

   yes, let cheat   no, don't let cheat   can't decide

7. In general, how important is it not to cheat? *(Circle one.)*

   very important   important   can't decide

8. Is it right for a teacher to punish cheaters? *(Circle one.)*

   yes, right   no, not right   can't decide

EQUIP for Educators: Teaching Youth (Grades 5–8) to Think and Act Responsibly © 2005 by A-M. DiBiase, J.C. Gibbs, and G.B. Potter. Champaign, IL: Research Press (800–519–2707; www.researchpress.com).

EDUCATOR NOTES
Alfonso's Problem Situation

KEY VALUE: HONESTY

Alfonso's Problem Situation returns to the theme of negative peer pressure, in this case from a friend who wants to cheat on a test. This problem situation is placed at the end of the social decision making curriculum component for a reason: At this point, the students' group culture may be positive enough to support the cultivation and consolidation of mature morality *even when it comes to cheating at school.*

Mature reasons are that it is unfair for Doug to get the benefit of Alfonso's work, that letting Doug cheat will encourage his attitude that he can let other people do his work for him (alert students will identify such an attitude as a Self-Centered thinking error), that Doug deserves to flunk and needs to learn a lesson, that Doug is hurting himself in the long run by cheating instead of learning, that Doug is also hurting his parents, and that the teacher has placed trust in Doug and Alfonso by putting them on their honor not to cheat. One cannot have a close relationship with a person who cheats (Question 5) because one never knows when the person might be planning to cheat you.

Pragmatic reasons for not letting Doug cheat might include the notion that the teacher could come back unexpectedly and catch both of them, and that if Doug is not caught, he might wind up with a grade higher than Alfonso's.

Alert students will likely identify the thinking errors in arguments in favor of letting Doug cheat: " There's nothing wrong with giving a little help to a friend"(Minimizing/Mislabeling) or "It is the teacher's fault for leaving the room" (Blaming Others).

Students who advocate cheating might acknowledge on Question 4 that they, as *teacher,* would not want Alfonso to let Doug cheat; they should be challenged to say that the teacher has a right to expect honesty. If so, then isn't their "cheating is okay" attitude Self-Centered and wrong?

Regina's Problem Situation

"Your father is late again," Regina's mother tells Regina one night as she sits down to dinner. Regina knows why. She passed her father's car on the way home from school. It was parked outside a tavern. Regina's mother and father have argued many times about her father's stopping off at a bar on his way home from work. After their last argument, her father promised he would never do it again. "I wonder why your father is late," Regina's mother says. "Do you think I should trust what he said about not drinking anymore? Do you think he stopped off at the bar again?"

What should Regina say or do?

1. Should Regina cover for her father by lying to her mother? *(Circle one.)*

   yes, should cover   no, should tell   can't decide
                              the truth

2. Was it right for Regina's mother to put Regina on the spot by asking her a question about her father? *(Circle one.)*

   yes, right   no, wrong   can't decide

3. What if Regina's father drinks a lot when he stops at the bar and then comes home and beats up on Regina's mother—and sometimes even Regina? Then what should Regina do? *(Circle one.)*

   cover for him   tell the truth   can't decide

4. Which is most important for Regina's decision? *(Circle one.)*

   what's best for herself   what's best for her mother

   what's best for her dad   what's best for the family

5. In general, how important is it to tell the truth? *(Circle one.)*

   very important   important   not important

EQUIP for Educators: Teaching Youth (Grades 5–8) to Think and Act Responsibly © 2005 by A-M. DiBiase, J.C. Gibbs, and G.B. Potter. Champaign, IL: Research Press (800–519–2707; www.researchpress.com).

EDUCATOR NOTES
Regina's Problem Situation

This problem situation is intended for more seriously at-risk students.

KEY VALUES: QUALITY OF LIFE AND TRUTH

Unique among the problem situations, Regina's Problem Situation concerns parental rather than peer pressure. Furthermore, whereas in peer situations the peer frequently has a negative or irresponsible aim, in Regina's Problem Situation the mother is at least well intentioned in her questions about the father.

This situation is problematic for students until Question 3 ("What if Regina's father drinks a lot when he stops at the bar and then comes home and beats up on Regina's mother—and sometimes even on Regina?"). Students here might indicate that Regina should tell her mother what he knows, in the interest of what is best for the family. (See also Question 4.) These questions plus Question 5 (concerning the importance of telling the truth) offer the best opportunities for cultivating and consolidating mature morality.

Dissenters might suggest that it was wrong for Regina's mother to put Regina on the spot (Question 2) and that getting Regina involved is too heavy a burden to place on a child—Regina would feel guilty if her disclosure resulted in a divorce. They may suggest that Regina could help in a limited way by having a private talk with her dad. Pragmatically, however, if Regina tells her mother (Question 1), her dad may become very angry with her.

Session/Skill _____ **Date** _____

Triad members _____

In General

☐ Yes ☐ No   1. Did triad members follow the ground rules (concerning listening, confidentiality, etc.)?

☐ Yes ☐ No   2. Were all triad members interested and involved?

   If not, list the names of uninvolved triad members:

   _____

   _____

   _____

☐ Yes ☐ No   3. Did you find some constructive value in every serious comment made by a triad member?

☐ Yes ☐ No   4. Did you maintain a normal voice volume and speak in a respectful rather than threatening or demanding tone?

☐ Yes ☐ No   5. Did you maintain a balance between criticism and approval by using the "sandwich" style of constructive criticism (in which a critical comment is preceded and followed by supportive ones)?

☐ Yes ☐ No   6. Did you appropriately use the ask, don't tell method?

For the Session

Phase 1: Introducing the Problem Situation

☐ Yes ☐ No   1. Did you make sure the triads understood the problem situation (e.g., "Who can tell the group just what Jerry's problem situation is? Why is that a problem?")?

EQUIP for Educators: Teaching Youth (Grades 5–8) to Think and Act Responsibly © 2005 by A-M. DiBiase, J. C. Gibbs, and G. B. Potter. Champaign, IL: Research Press (800–519–2707; www.researchpress.com).

Educator's Review: Mature Moral Judgment (continued)

☐ Yes ☐ No   2. Did you relate the problem situation to triad members' everyday lives (e.g., "Do problems like this happen? Who has been in a situation like this? Tell the group about it.")?

Phase 2: Cultivating Mature Morality

☐ Yes ☐ No   3. Did you establish mature morality as the tone for the rest of the session (e.g., eliciting and listing on the easel pad reasons for each positive majority decision)?

☐ Yes ☐ No   4. Did you support and relabel the "should" as strong (e.g., "Yes, it does take guts to do the right thing")?

Phase 3: Remediating Moral Developmental Delay

☐ Yes ☐ No   5. Did you use more mature triad members and their reasons (Phase 2) to challenge the hedonistic or pragmatic arguments of some triad members?

☐ Yes ☐ No   6. Did you create role-taking opportunities in other ways as well (e.g., "What would the world be like if everybody did that?"; "How would you feel if you were Bruno?")?

Phase 4: Consolidating Mature Morality

☐ Yes ☐ No   7. Did you make positive decisions and mature reasons unanimous for the group (e.g., "Any strong objections if I circle that decision as the group decision/underline that reason as the group's number one reason?")

☐ Yes ☐ No   8. Did you praise the group for its positive decisions and mature reasons (e.g., "I'm really pleased that the group was able to name so many good, strong decisions and back them up with good, strong reasons"; "Would the group like to tape this sheet onto the wall?")?

Post-Meeting

☐ Yes ☐ No   9. Did you make notes regarding the session and individual group members?

CHAPTER
6 FINAL SESSION AND CONCLUSION

Just as a preliminary session introduces the *EQUIP for Educators* curriculum and its thinking errors vocabulary to students (see chapter 2), a final session concludes the program. This final session provides an opportunity for an overall review of the curriculum. This review helps students consolidate their learning.

You may wish to treat this concluding session as a kind of graduation ceremony for the students. Following the Up or Down? review exercise shown in Figure 6.1, you might distribute certificates like the example in Figure 6.2 and make appropriate motivational comments that remind students of the introductory remarks you made before the start of the curriculum. You should stress the importance of students' continuing to practice the things they have learned.

This chapter concludes not only the EQUIP curriculum for your students, but also this book. We wish you the best in your important work of primary and secondary prevention. We hope that *EQUIP for Educators* will help move your at-risk students toward responsible thinking and acting. In that way, they will help themselves—and will contribute toward making this world a home that we can legitimately call Planet B.

Up or Down?

Student _____ Date _____

Check the correct response. **Up** *is responsible, and* **Down** *is irresponsible.*

Thought, Skill, or Behavior

	Up	Down
1. Planet A	☐	☐
2. Noticing an early warning sign of anger	☐	☐
3. Constructively expressing a complaint	☐	☐
4. Apologizing if you're partly responsible for a problem	☐	☐
5. Stealing and thinking it's okay because you didn't steal from anyone you knew	☐	☐
6. Caring for someone who is sad or upset	☐	☐
7. Using put-downs and threats	☐	☐
8. Stealing something from a car with the excuse that the owner left it unlocked	☐	☐
9. Taking deep breaths when angry	☐	☐
10. Making a Self-Centered thinking error	☐	☐
11. Doing it for others only if they will do it for you	☐	☐
12. Preparing for a stressful conversation	☐	☐
13. Selling harmful drugs	☐	☐
14. Giving in to peer pressure to hurt someone	☐	☐
15. Suggesting a responsible alternative to a negative act your friends want you to do	☐	☐
16. Responding constructively to others' anger	☐	☐
17. Thinking ahead to consequences	☐	☐
18. Using self-evaluation	☐	☐

EQUIP for Educators: Teaching Youth (Grades 5–8) to Think and Act Responsibly © 2005 by A-M. DiBiase, J. C. Gibbs, and G. B. Potter. Champaign, IL: Research Press (800–519–2707; www.researchpress.com).

(page 1 of 2)   **201**

Figure 6.1   Up or Down?

Up or Down? (continued)

19. Using "I" statements	❑	❑
20. Keeping out of fights	❑	❑
21. Victimizing others and using the excuse that you were a victim	❑	❑
22. Delivering drugs for a friend	❑	❑
23. Blaming the victim	❑	❑
24. Thinking whether the person is right when you are accused of something	❑	❑
25. Expressing care and appreciation	❑	❑
26. Not telling on a suicidal friend	❑	❑
27. Responding constructively to failure	❑	❑
28. Helping a friend cheat	❑	❑
29. Showing how you would want to be treated by the way you treat others	❑	❑
30. Planet B	❑	❑

202   *(page 2 of 2)*

Figure 6.1   Up or Down? (continued)

EQUIP
Certificate

This certificate is presented to

_____

Awarded for completion of an Anger
Management, Social Skills, and
Social Decision Making Program

Presented by _____

Date _____

EQUIP for Educators: Teaching Youth (Grades 5–8) to Think and Act Responsibly © 2005 by A-M. DiBiase,
J. C. Gibbs, and G. B. Potter. Champaign, IL: Research Press (800–519–2707; www.researchpress.com).

Figure 6.2   EQUIP Certificate

FINAL SESSION

Up or Down?

OVERVIEW OF EXPECTATIONS AND ACTIVITIES

Students will . . .

♦ Review and have the opportunity to answer questions about thoughts, skills, and behaviors spanning all three *EQUIP for Educators* curriculum components

♦ Test their knowledge relating to curriculum content

♦ Receive encouragement to use concepts and skills learned in the curriculum to help themselves and others

The Up or Down? student handout may be distributed before or during the session. Either way, students should be reminded not to share their answers.

PROCEDURE AND EDUCATOR NOTES

Introduce the session by letting group members know that this activity provides a review of what has been discussed during the curriculum sessions. Explain that the concept "up or down" can be used to describe thoughts, skills, or behaviors. *Up* equals positive or responsible. *Down* equals negative or irresponsible.

Tell group members that they have been learning about two kinds of lives:

The Planet A life involves victimizing, which is destructive and in which you hurt other people and yourself. This life pulls everyone *Down!*

The Planet B life is constructive and responsible. It involves helping other people and yourself. This life lifts everyone *Up!*

Let students know that each person is responsible for choosing the type of life he or she will live. The truly strong people choose to live a positive and constructive life that lifts them up and gains them respect from their family, friends, and other people.

Lead the students through the list on the Up or Down? review exercise, encouraging discussion of each item. Emphasize the areas that the group or individuals may have struggled with during previous sessions. Verbally reward the group and/or individuals for their strength and willingness to change. Emphasize that it is very important for students to continue to practice the strategies they have learned.

APPENDIX

REPRODUCIBLE MATERIALS FOR STUDENTS

Ground Rules for EQUIP Discussions

1. *Attend to the speaker.*

2. *Each student must be involved and participate.*

3. *Only one student talks at a time.*

4. *Listen to the other person who is talking.*

5. *If you disagree with someone, do so respectfully.*

6. *If you criticize a fellow student, give him or her a chance to respond.*

7. *Never put down or threaten anyone.*

8. *Stay focused on the subject.*

9. *Remember who said what.*

10. *Everything personal that is shared in the room, stays in the room.*

EQUIP for Educators: Teaching Youth (Grades 5–8) to Think and Act Responsibly © 2005 by A-M. DiBiase, J. C. Gibbs, and G. B. Potter. Champaign, IL: Research Press (800–519–2707; www.researchpress.com).

Thinking Errors Grid

A. Self-Centered	**B. Minimizing/Mislabeling**
C. Assuming the Worst	**D. Blaming Others**

Thinking Errors Definitions

## A. Self-Centered	Self-Centered thinking means that you think your opinions and feelings are more important than the opinions and feelings of other people. You may not even consider how another person might feel about things. Self-Centered thinking can also mean that you think only about what you want right now and do not think about how your behaviors will affect you or others in the future.
## B. Minimizing/Mislabeling	Minimizing/Mislabeling means that you think your problems or behaviors are not as wrong or harmful as they really are. You put a label on your bad behavior to make it sound okay or good, or you describe someone with a bad name (like *snitch* or *fool*) so it will seem okay to hurt the person.
## C. Assuming the Worst	Assuming the Worst means that you think everyone is out to get you (or someone else). *(Example:* If someone accidentally bumps into you in the hall, you assume the person did it on purpose instead of thinking it was an accident.) Assuming the Worst about yourself means that you think only bad things can happen to you and that you can't do anything about it. Assuming the Worst can also mean that you think you or other people will not be able to change or make improvements or do anything about bad things that happen in life.
## D. Blaming Others	Blaming Others means that you do not take responsibility for your own behavior, but instead blame other people for harmful behavior when it is really your fault. You may think you can harm innocent others—that they deserve it because people in the past treated you badly. Blaming Others can also mean that you think your bad behaviors are okay because you were on drugs or alcohol or in a bad mood.

EQUIP for Educators: Teaching Youth (Grades 5–8) to Think and Act Responsibly © 2005 by A-M. DiBiase, J. C. Gibbs, and G. B. Potter. Champaign, IL: Research Press (800–519–2707; www.researchpress.com).

Thinking Errors Question Cards

1. Sometimes you have to lie to get what you want.

2. If I see something I like, I take it.

3. When I get mad, I don't care who gets hurt.

4. If I really want something, it doesn't matter how I get it.

5. You should get what you need, even if it means someone has to get hurt.

6. Rules are mostly meant for other people.

7. Getting what you need is the only important thing.

8. If I lied to someone, that's my business.

9. If I made a mistake, it's because I got mixed up with the wrong crowd.

10. If someone leaves a car unlocked, they are asking to have it stolen.

11. It's okay to tell a lie if someone is dumb enough to fall for it.

12. People force you to lie if they ask too many questions.

EQUIP for Educators: Teaching Youth (Grades 5–8) to Think and Act Responsibly © 2005 by A-M. DiBiase, J. C. Gibbs, and G. B. Potter. Champaign, IL: Research Press (800–519–2707; www.researchpress.com).

(page 1 of 3)

Thinking Errors Question Cards (continued)

13. People are always trying to start fights with me.

14. If someone is careless enough to lose a wallet, they deserve to have it stolen.

15. If people don't cooperate with me, it's not my fault if someone gets hurt.

16. When I lose my temper, it's because people try to make me mad.

17. People need to be roughed up once in a while.

18. You have to get even with people who don't show you respect.

19. Everybody lies—it's no big deal.

20. If you know you can get away with it, only a fool wouldn't steal.

21. Only a coward would ever walk away from a fight.

22. Stores make enough money that it's OK to just take things you need.

23. A lie doesn't really matter if you don't know that person.

24. Everybody breaks the law—it's no big deal.

25. I can't help losing my temper a lot.	26. You can't trust people because they will always lie to you.
27. It's no use trying to stay out of fights.	28. No matter how hard I try, I can't help getting in trouble.
29. If you don't push people around, you will always get picked on.	30. You might as well steal. If *you* don't take it, somebody else will.
31. I might as well lie—when I tell the truth, people don't believe me anyway.	32. Everybody steals—you might as well get your share.

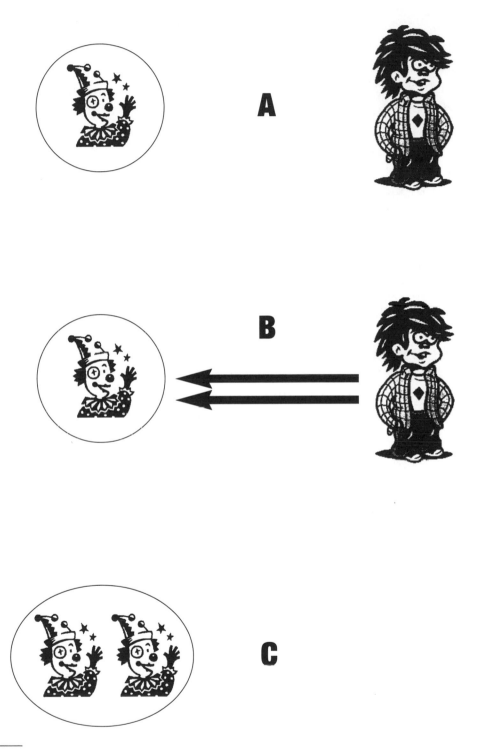

EQUIP for Educators: Teaching Youth (Grades 5–8) to Think and Act Responsibly © 2005 by A-M. DiBiase, J. C. Gibbs, and G. B. Potter. Champaign, IL: Research Press (800–519–2707; www.researchpress.com).

John's Thinking Errors

Triad members _____ **Date** _____

John is in the kitchen of his apartment. John's wife, Meagan, is angry at him for something he did to hurt her. She yells at him. She pushes his shoulder. Thoughts run through John's head. John does nothing to correct the errors in his thoughts. John becomes furious. He screams at Meagan. John picks up a book nearby and throws it at her.

1. What thoughts, do you think, ran through John's head, both during the situation and afterward? Suggest some sample thoughts.

2. What are the errors in these thoughts? Remember that Meagan was mad at John because he had done something to hurt her. What do you think that might have been?

3. What might John have told himself in this situation? In other words, how might John have "talked back" to his thinking errors? Suggest some things John could have said to himself to correct each type of thinking error.

4. If John had corrected his thinking errors, would he still have thrown the book?

EQUIP for Educators: Teaching Youth (Grades 5–8) to Think and Act Responsibly © 2005 by A-M. DiBiase, J. C. Gibbs, and G. B. Potter. Champaign, IL: Research Press (800–519–2707; www.researchpress.com).

Problem Names and Thinking Errors

Student _____ **Date** _____

Social/behavioral problems are actions that cause harm to oneself, others, or property.

A. Has someone else's problem(s) ever hurt you?   Yes   No

Think of a time that someone's problem(s) have hurt you. Choose the best name for that problem from the list below and write it here.

_____

B. Have your problem(s) ever hurt someone else?   Yes   No

Think of a time your problem hurt someone else. Choose the best name for that problem from the list below and write it here.

_____

GENERAL PROBLEMS

The first three problems are general problems. These general problems may be related to any of the specific problems. When you use one of the general problem names to describe a behavior, to get a good understanding of the situation you must also name one of the specific problems (Numbers 4–12).

1. Low Self-Image

The person has a poor opinion of himself or herself. Often feels put down or of no worth. Quits easily. Plays "poor me" or perceives self as victim even when victimizing others. Feels accepted only by others who also feel bad about themselves.

Briefly describe a situation in which you or someone you know showed a Low Self-Image problem.

_____

_____

Was a specific problem shown at the same time?   Yes   No

What was the problem?

_____

EQUIP for Educators: Teaching Youth (Grades 5–8) to Think and Act Responsibly © 2005 by A-M. DiBiase, J. C. Gibbs, and G. B. Potter. Champaign, IL: Research Press (800–519–2707; www.researchpress.com).

Problem Names and Thinking Errors (continued)

2. Inconsiderate of Self

The person does things that are damaging to himself or herself. He or she tries to run from problems or deny them.

Briefly describe a situation in which you or someone you know showed an Inconsiderate of Self problem.

_____

_____

Was a specific problem shown at the same time?   Yes   No

What was the problem?

_____

3. Inconsiderate of Others

The person does things that are harmful to others. Doesn't care about needs or feelings of others. Enjoys putting people down or laughing at them. Takes advantage of weaker persons or those with problems.

Briefly describe a situation in which you or someone you know showed an Inconsiderate of Others problem.

_____

_____

Was a specific problem shown at the same time?   Yes   No

What was the problem?

_____

Problem Names and Thinking Errors (continued)

SPECIFIC PROBLEMS

4. Authority Problem

The person gets into major confrontations with teachers, parents, and others in authority, often over minor matters. Resents anyone telling him or her what to do or even giving advice. Won't listen.

I know someone who has this problem.	Yes	No
I have this problem.	Yes	No

5. Easily Angered

The person quickly takes offense, is easily frustrated or irritated, and throws tantrums.

I know someone who has this problem.	Yes	No
I have this problem.	Yes	No

6. Aggravates Others

The person threatens, bullies, hassles, teases, or uses put-downs to hurt other people. "Pays back" even when others didn't mean to put the person down.

I know someone who has this problem.	Yes	No
I have this problem.	Yes	No

7. Misleads Others

The person manipulates others into doing his or her dirty work; will abandon them if they are caught.

I know someone who has this problem.	Yes	No
I have this problem.	Yes	No

8. Easily Misled

The person prefers to associate with irresponsible peers, is easily drawn into their antisocial behavior. Is willing to be their flunky—hopes to gain their approval.

I know someone who has this problem.	Yes	No
I have this problem.	Yes	No

Problem Names and Thinking Errors (continued)

9. Alcohol or Drug Problem

The person misuses substances that can hurt him or her and is afraid he or she will not have friends otherwise. Is afraid to face life without a crutch. Avoids issues and people through substance abuse. Usually is very self-centered and minimizes the use of drugs by saying they are not bad or are within his or her control. When the person does something wrong, he or she blames the drugs by saying, "I was high—I couldn't help it."

I know someone who has this problem.   Yes   No

I have this problem.   Yes   No

10. Stealing

The person takes things that belong to others. Does not respect others. Is willing to hurt another person to take what he or she wants.

I know someone who has this problem.   Yes   No

I have this problem.   Yes   No

11. Lying

The person cannot be trusted to tell the truth or the whole story. Twists the truth to create a false impression. Denies everything when he or she thinks it is possible to get away with it. Finds it exciting to scheme and then get away with a lie. May lie even when there is nothing to be gained.

I know someone who has this problem.   Yes   No

I have this problem.   Yes   No

12. Fronting

The person tries to impress others, puts on an act, clowns around to get attention. Is afraid to show his or her true feelings.

I know someone who has this problem.   Yes   No

I have this problem.   Yes   No

How many problems do you have? _____

What are your most serious problems? _____

Problem Names and Thinking Errors (continued)

Number 1 problem? _____

Number 2 problem? _____

Number 3 problem? _____

By correctly identifying your problems, you have taken a big step in helping yourself. Save this handout to use later in the program. You may find it very useful.

Thinking Errors

The following terms are used to identify thinking errors. These terms are used throughout the program. When you name your behavioral problem, the thinking error that caused it is also named. *Remember: It is your thinking error that led to your social/behavioral problem.*

THE PRIMARY THINKING ERROR

1. Self-Centered

Self-Centered thinking means that you think your opinions and feelings are more important than the opinions and feelings of other people. Self-Centered is the primary, or basic, thinking error. The Self-Centered thinking error can severely limit one person's consideration for the viewpoint of another person.

Does someone you know seem to have a Self-Centered thinking error? How do you know? Explain without using the person's name.

_____

_____

_____

It is important to understand that a person's thoughts cannot be known by anyone other than that person. You can guess what a person is thinking, but you will not know for sure until that person shares his or her thoughts.

Has anyone ever said to you, "I know what you are thinking," but then was wrong? Explain.

_____

_____

_____

If you want to know what another person is thinking, what do you have to do?

_____

Problem Names and Thinking Errors (continued)

SECONDARY THINKING ERRORS

The Self-Centered person uses other (secondary) thinking errors to avoid feeling bad (guilt, remorse, low self-concept) about his or her bad (antisocial) behavior and to allow the selfish thoughts and behaviors to continue. For example, a 17-year-old used a secondary thinking error (Blaming Others) to make himself feel better about breaking into people's homes. He said, "If I started feeling bad, I'd say, 'Tough rocks for him. He should have had his house locked better and the alarm on.'" The Self-Centered person almost always shows his or her basic Self-Centered thinking error *and* one of the following secondary thinking errors.

2. Minimizing/Mislabeling

Example: "He was a fool and got jumped." What really happened: "I punched and kicked him because he told his neighbor the truth, that I was the person who stole the neighbor's stereo." Or what really happened: The young man was brutally beaten because he told the principal that someone had a gun and threatened some other kids.

Write another example and explain.

_____

_____

_____

3. Assuming the Worst

Example: Someone left a CD player and headphones on the library table. You think that you should take them for yourself because if you don't, someone else will.

Write another example and explain.

_____

_____

_____

Problem Names and Thinking Errors (continued)

4. Blaming Others

Example: "I got mixed up with the wrong people." What really happened: You agreed to help your friend take something that belonged to someone else.

Write another example and explain.

_____

_____

_____

Are thinking and behaving connected? Explain.

_____

_____

_____

How many thinking errors do you have? _____

What are your most common thinking errors? _____

Number 1 thinking error _____

Number 2 thinking error _____

Number 3 thinking error _____

By identifying your thinking errors, you have taken a big step in helping yourself to correct faulty thinking. It takes a strong person to admit to thinking errors and the behavioral problems they cause.

Self-Help Log A: Problems and Thinking Errors

Student _____ Date _____

_____ Morning _____ Afternoon _____ Evening

Where were you?

_____ Class _____ Gym _____ Hall _____ In class/session

What kind of problems did you have?

_____ Low Self-Image	_____ Easily Angered	_____ Alcohol or Drug Problem
_____ Inconsiderate of Self	_____ Aggravates Others	_____ Stealing
_____ Inconsiderate of Others	_____ Misleads Others	_____ Lying
_____ Authority Problem	_____ Easily Misled	_____ Fronting

You had this/these problems because of what kind of thinking error?

_____ Self-Centered	_____ Assuming the Worst
_____ Minimizing/Mislabeling	_____ Blaming Others

Describe the problems.

What were you thinking (describe the thinking error)?

How angry were you?

1	2	3	4	5
Burning mad	Really angry	Moderately angry	Mildly angry	Not angry at all

How did you handle yourself?

1	2	3	4	5
Poorly	Not so well	Okay	Well	Great

I will not have this/these problem(s) in the future if I . . . .

EQUIP for Educators: Teaching Youth (Grades 5–8) to Think and Act Responsibly © 2005 by A-M. DiBiase, J. C. Gibbs, and G. B. Potter. Champaign, IL: Research Press (800–519–2707; www.researchpress.com).

Self-Help Log B: Positive Behaviors
(Structured Version)

Student _____ **Date** _____

_____ Morning _____ Afternoon _____ Evening

	Yes	No
1. I completed my assigned homework.	___	___
2. I followed the classroom rules.	___	___
3. I contributed to my triad work in class.	___	___
4. I did the assigned work in class.	___	___
5. I accepted constructive criticism.	___	___
6. I stood up for my rights in a positive way.	___	___
7. I accepted responsibility for my actions and did not make excuses.	___	___
8. I talked a peer out of verbally or physically fighting.	___	___
9. I complimented someone for something that person did.	___	___
10. I showed consideration for another.	___	___
11. I _____ .		

EQUIP for Educators: Teaching Youth (Grades 5–8) to Think and Act Responsibly © 2005 by A-M. DiBiase,
J. C. Gibbs, and G. B. Potter. Champaign, IL: Research Press (800–519–2707; www.researchpress.com).

Self-Help Log C: Positive Behaviors
(Open-Ended Version)

Student _____ Date _____

What did you do to help yourself today?

What did you do to help someone else today?

———————

EQUIP for Educators: Teaching Youth (Grades 5–8) to Think and Act Responsibly © 2005 by A-M. DiBiase, J. C. Gibbs, and G. B. Potter. Champaign, IL: Research Press (800–519–2707; www.researchpress.com).

Things You Do That Make Other People Angry

Student _____ **Date** _____

List two things you do that make other people angry or two things you have
done that made someone else feel hurt or angry.

1. _____

   _____

   _____

2. _____

   _____

   _____

Practice Reversing

Triad members _____ Date _____

Situation 1

A student says:

I don't have any problems. You jerks are the ones with the problem. The only problem I have is you dummies keep hassling me.

You say:

You know, it'll be great when you get the courage to face your problems. Then you'll thank people trying to help you instead of putting them down and blaming them.

Situation 2

A student says:

I got in trouble because both my parents are alcoholics and don't care about me.

You say:

You mean that all people with parents who have problems go out and hurt people?

Situation 3

A student says:

It's all my mother's fault. They never would have caught me if she didn't tell the police I was stealing.

You say:

Did your mother do the stealing? Did anyone force you to steal? No? So whose fault is it, really, that you stole?

Situation 4

A student says:

My friends talked me into it—it's their fault. I just got mixed up with the wrong people.

You say:

_____

_____

EQUIP for Educators: Teaching Youth (Grades 5–8) to Think and Act Responsibly © 2005 by A-M. DiBiase, J. C. Gibbs, and G. B. Potter. Champaign, IL: Research Press (800–519–2707; www.researchpress.com).

Practice Reversing (continued)

Situation 5

A student says:

I don't feel like playing basketball. They never pass me the ball.

You say:

_____

_____

Situation 6

A student says:

He was asking for it. He kept teasing me.

You say:

_____

_____

Situation 7

A student says:

I got in trouble because both my parents did drugs and neglected me.

You say:

_____

_____

Victims and Victimizers

Triad members _____ **Date** _____

You are staying at your grandparents' home for the weekend. Your grandparents have lived in that home for many years. You arrive home with your grandparents from dinner. When you open the front door, you see that the house has been broken into. Many of your grandparents' things have been thrown all around. Their crystal glasses have been smashed. Their family photo album has been destroyed. Some of their things, like a wedding ring that belonged to your great-grandmother, have been stolen.

1. What would be the first thing that you would do?

2. How do you think you would be feeling? Have you ever had anything stolen from you? How did you feel? Does that help you understand how your grandparents feel?

3. Would you leave your grandparents in the house alone for the night? Why or why not? Do you think your grandparents would feel afraid or worried? When have you felt afraid or worried? Does that help you understand how your grandparents would feel?

4. Do you think your grandparents will get their things back?

5. Who are the victims in this situation? Can you think of any long-term or indirect victims? (List some ways that victims suffer: in body, in mind, in money, in daily living, with their friends.)

6. Who are the main victimizers in this situation? If a victimizer were to think ahead to the many ways a victim would suffer, would the victimizer still go ahead and do the crime?

7. Have you ever been made a victim? By whom? Have you victimized others? Whom have you victimized? Do most people who have been victimized go on to victimize others? Which have you been more of, victim or victimizer?

EQUIP for Educators: Teaching Youth (Grades 5–8) to Think and Act Responsibly © 2005 by A-M. DiBiase, J. C. Gibbs, and G. B. Potter. Champaign, IL: Research Press (800–519–2707; www.researchpress.com).

Social Skills Practice Sheet

Student _____ **Date** _____

Practice assignment

Skill _____

If applicable:

Use with whom? _____

Use when? _____

Use where? _____

Describe what happened when you did the practice assignment. For example, did you skip any steps? What was the other person's reaction?

_____

_____

_____

Rate yourself on how well you used the skill. (Check one.)

___ Excellent   ___ Good   ___ Fair   ___ Poor

EQUIP for Educators: Teaching Youth (Grades 5–8) to Think and Act Responsibly © 2005 by A-M. DiBiase, J. C. Gibbs, and G. B. Potter. Champaign, IL: Research Press (800–519–2707; www.researchpress.com).

Keys to Good Listening

Student _____ Date _____

1. **Look at the person.**

2. **Let the person finish speaking.**

3. **Say something to show you are listening.**

4. **Give a brief encouragement.**

   Yeah.

   Really?

   Hmm.

   Wow!

   Cool!

5. **Ask a question to show you would like to know more.**

   What happened next?

   How did you do that?

   Where did you go?

   What did you do then?

6. **Sum up what the person is saying.**

   It sounds like you . . . .

   From what you said, it seems that . . . .

   So you think that . . . .

   In other words, you . . . .

EQUIP for Educators: Teaching Youth (Grades 5–8) to Think and Act Responsibly © 2005 by A-M. DiBiase, J. C. Gibbs, and G. B. Potter. Champaign, IL: Research Press (800–519–2707; www.researchpress.com).

Nonlistening Behaviors

Student _____ Date _____

1. Changing the subject

2. Trying to make a joke out of something

3. Giving advice

4. Ignoring or fidgeting

5. Not looking at the speaker

6. Turning your body away from the speaker

7. Laughing inappropriately

8. Interrupting by saying things like "You think that's great, you should hear what I did," or "That reminds me of the time . . . ."

9. Looking bored

10. Saying, "Yeah, Yeah, Yeah," as if you want the speaker to hurry

11. Playing with paper or other things

_____

EQUIP for Educators: Teaching Youth (Grades 5–8) to Think and Act Responsibly © 2005 by A-M. DiBiase, J. C. Gibbs, and G. B. Potter. Champaign, IL: Research Press (800–519–2707; www.researchpress.com).

How Well Did You Listen?

Student _____ Date _____

Put a check mark next to the things you did while you were listening.

_____ I sat quietly while the speaker was talking.

_____ I ignored the distractions.

_____ I faced the speaker.

_____ I watched the speaker's expression.

_____ I thought about what the speaker was saying and not just about what I wanted to say.

_____ I nodded my head now and then to show I was interested in what the speaker was saying.

_____ I made little comments to show I was listening.

_____ I asked questions to encourage the speaker to tell me more.

_____ I let the speaker finish talking before I asked a question.

_____ I summed up what the speaker said.

One of the things I could have done a little better is _____.

EQUIP for Educators: Teaching Youth (Grades 5–8) to Think and Act Responsibly © 2005 by A-M. DiBiase, J. C. Gibbs, and G. B. Potter. Champaign, IL: Research Press (800–519–2707; www.researchpress.com).

Up or Down?

Student _____ Date _____

Check the correct response. **Up** *is responsible, and* **Down** *is irresponsible.*

Thought, Skill, or Behavior

	Up	Down
1. Planet A	❏	❏
2. Noticing an early warning sign of anger	❏	❏
3. Constructively expressing a complaint	❏	❏
4. Apologizing if you're partly responsible for a problem	❏	❏
5. Stealing and thinking it's okay because you didn't steal from anyone you knew	❏	❏
6. Caring for someone who is sad or upset	❏	❏
7. Using put-downs and threats	❏	❏
8. Stealing something from a car with the excuse that the owner left it unlocked	❏	❏
9. Taking deep breaths when angry	❏	❏
10. Making a Self-Centered thinking error	❏	❏
11. Doing it for others only if they will do it for you	❏	❏
12. Preparing for a stressful conversation	❏	❏
13. Selling harmful drugs	❏	❏
14. Giving in to peer pressure to hurt someone	❏	❏
15. Suggesting a responsible alternative to a negative act your friends want you to do	❏	❏
16. Responding constructively to others' anger	❏	❏
17. Thinking ahead to consequences	❏	❏
18. Using self-evaluation	❏	❏

Up or Down? (continued)

19. Using "I" statements ☐ ☐

20. Keeping out of fights ☐ ☐

21. Victimizing others and using the excuse that you were a victim ☐ ☐

22. Delivering drugs for a friend ☐ ☐

23. Blaming the victim ☐ ☐

24. Thinking whether the person is right when you are accused of something ☐ ☐

25. Expressing care and appreciation ☐ ☐

26. Not telling on a suicidal friend ☐ ☐

27. Responding constructively to failure ☐ ☐

28. Helping a friend cheat ☐ ☐

29. Showing how you would want to be treated by the way you treat others ☐ ☐

30. Planet B ☐ ☐

EQUIP

Certificate

This certificate is presented to

_____

Awarded for completion of an Anger Management, Social Skills, and Social Decision Making Program

Presented by _____

Date _____

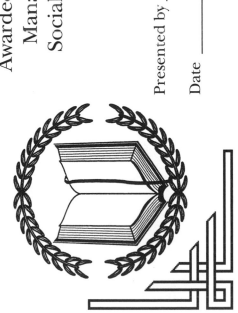

References

Amendola, A.M., & Oliver, R.W. (2003). LSCI and Aggression Replacement Training: A multi-modal approach. *Reclaiming Children and Youth, 12,* 181–185.

Barriga, A.Q., Gibbs, J.C., Potter, G.B., & Liau, A.K. (2001). *How I Think (HIT) Questionnaire manual.* Champaign, IL: Research Press.

Beck, A.T. (1999). *Prisoners of hate: The cognitive basis of anger, hostility, and violence.* New York: Discovery Channel.

Berkowitz, M.W., & Bier, M.C. (in press). *What can work in character education?* Washington, DC: Character Education Partnership.

Carducci, D. J. (1980). Positive Peer Culture and assertive training: Complementary modalities for dealing with disturbed and disturbing adolescents in the classroom. *Behavioral Disorders, 5,* 156–162.

Damon, W. (1995). *Greater expectations: Overcoming the culture of indulgence in America's homes and schools.* New York: Free Press.

DiBiase, A-M. (2002). Equipping children to think and behave responsibly: An evaluation of a multi-component cognitive-developmental program. *Dissertation Abstracts International, 63*(5), 442 (UMI No. 3052505).

Ellis, A. (1977). Rational-emotive therapy: Research data that support the clinical and personality hypothesis of RET and other modes of cognitive-behavior therapy. *Counseling Psychologist, 7,* 2–42.

Feindler, E.L., & Ecton, R.R. (1986). *Adolescent anger control: Cognitive-behavioral techniques.* New York: Pergamon.

Gibbs, J.C. (2003). *Moral development and reality: Beyond the theories of Kohlberg and Hoffman.* Thousand Oaks, CA: Sage.

Gibbs, J.C. (2004). The moral reasoning training component. In A.P. Goldstein, R. Nensen, M. Kalt, & B. Daleford (Eds.), *New perspectives in Aggression Replacement Training* (pp. 51–72). Chichester, UK: Wiley & Sons.

Gibbs, J.C., Barriga, A.Q., & Potter, G.B. (2001). *How I Think (HIT) Questionnaire.* Champaign, IL: Research Press.

Gibbs, J.C., Basinger, K.S., & Fuller, D. (1992). *Moral maturity: Measuring the development of sociomoral reflection.* Hillsdale, NJ: Erlbaum.

Gibbs, J.C., Potter, G.B., & Goldstein, A.P. (1995). *The EQUIP program: Teaching youth to think and act responsibly through a peer-helping approach.* Champaign, IL: Research Press.

Gibbs, J.C., Swillinger, A., Leeman, L.W., Simonian, S.S., Rowland, S., & Jaycox, C. (1995). *Inventory of Adolescent Problems–Short Form (IAP–SF).* In J.C. Gibbs, G.B. Potter, & A.P. Goldstein, *The EQUIP program* (pp. 293–328). Champaign, IL: Research Press.

Goldstein, A.P. (1993). Interpersonal skills training interventions. In A.P. Goldstein & C.R. Huff (Eds.), *The gang intervention handbook* (pp. 87–157). Champaign, IL: Research Press.

Goldstein, A.P. (1999). *The Prepare Curriculum: Teaching prosocial competencies* (Rev. ed.). Champaign, IL: Research Press.

Goldstein, A.P., Glick, B., & Gibbs, J.C. (1998). *Aggression Replacement Training: A comprehensive intervention for aggressive youth* (Rev. ed.). Champaign, IL: Research Press.

Gregg, V., Gibbs, J.C., & Basinger, K.S. (1994). Patterns of delay in male and female delinquents' moral judgment. *Merrill-Palmer Quarterly, 40,* 538–553.

Gresham, F.M., & Elliot, S.N. (1990). *Social skills rating system manual.* Circle Pines, MN: American Guidance Service.

Horn, M., Shively, R., & Gibbs, J.C. (2005). *EQUIPPED for Life: A game for helping youth think and act responsibly* (2nd ed.). Champaign, IL: Research Press.

Kohlberg, L. (1984). *The psychology of moral development: Essays on moral development* (Vol. 2). San Francisco: Harper and Row.

Kohlberg, L., & Higgins, A. (1987). School democracy and social interaction. In W.M. Kurtines & J.L. Gewirtz (Eds.), *Moral development through social interaction* (pp. 102–128). New York: Wiley-Interscience.

Krevans, J., & Gibbs, J.C. (1996). Children's use of inductive discipline: Relations to children's empathy and prosocial behavior. *Child Development, 67,* 3264–3277.

Lickona, T. (1983). *Raising good children.* Toronto: Bantam.

Lickona, T. (2004). *Character matters: How to help our children develop good judgment, integrity, and other essential virtues.* New York: Simon and Schuster.

McGinnis, E. (2003). Aggression Replacement Training: A viable alternative. *Reclaiming Children and Youth, 12,* 161–166.

McGinnis, E., & Goldstein, A.P. (1997). *Skillstreaming the elementary school child: New strategies and perspectives for teaching prosocial skills* (Rev. ed.). Champaign, IL: Research Press.

Nelson, W.M., & Finch, A.J. (2000). *Children's Inventory of Anger.* Los Angeles: Western Psychological Services.

Office of Justice Programs. (2000). *Office of Juvenile Justice Programs resource guide* (3rd ed.). Washington, DC: U.S. Department of Justice.

Palmer, E.J., & Hollin, C.R. (1998). A comparison of patterns of moral development in young offenders and non-offenders. *Legal and Criminological Psychology, 3,* 225-235.

Piaget, J. (1965). *Moral judgment of the child* (M. Gabain, Trans.). New York: Free Press. (Original work published 1932)

Redl, F., & Wineman, D. (1951). *Children who hate.* Glencoe, IL: Free Press.

Salmon, S. (2003). Teaching empathy: The PEACE curriculum. *Reclaiming Children and Youth, 12,* 167–173.

Samenow, S.E. (1984). *Inside the criminal mind.* New York: Random House.

Thornton, T.N., Dahlberg, L.L., Lynch, B.S., & Baer, K. (2000). *Best practices of youth violence prevention: A sourcebook for community action.* Atlanta: Centers for Disease Control and Prevention, Division of Violence Prevention.

Vorrath, H.H., & Brendtro, L.K. (1985). *Positive peer culture* (2nd ed.). Hawthorne, NY: Aldine.

Yochelson, S., & Samenow, S.E. (1976). *The criminal personality: Vol 1. A profile for change.* New York: Jason Aronson.

Yochelson, S., & Samenow, S.E. (1977). *The criminal personality: Vol 2. The change process.* New York: Jason Aronson.

Yochelson, S., & Samenow, S.E. (1986). *The criminal personality: Vol 3. The drug user.* Northvale, NJ: Jason Aronson.

ABOUT THE AUTHORS

Ann-Marie DiBiase, Ph.D. (University at Buffalo, The State University of New York, 2002), is an assistant professor of educational psychology at Brock University, St. Catharines, Ontario. Her research has concerned cognitive-developmental theory, aggressive/antisocial behavior in children and youth, prevention/intervention programs for children at risk for antisocial behavior, moral development and assessment, and social cognition. A certified elementary school teacher, she has served as editor for two books and published articles in professional journals in these domains of study. She teaches graduate and undergraduate courses in educational psychology, behavioral disorders, and research design and methods.

John C. Gibbs, Ph.D. (Harvard University, 1972), is a professor of developmental psychology at The Ohio State University. He has been a member of the State of Ohio Governor's Council on Juvenile Justice and is a faculty associate of The Ohio State University Criminal Justice Research Center. His work has concerned development theory, assessment of social cognition and moral judgment development, and interventions with conduct-disordered adolescents. His authored or co-authored books include *Moral Development and Reality: Beyond the Theories of Kohlberg and Hoffman* and *Moral Maturity: Measuring the Development of Sociomoral Reflection.*

Granville Bud Potter, M.Ed. (Bowling Green State University, 1975), is currently the executive director of the Franklin County (Ohio) Community-Based Correction Facility. While serving in this capacity, he has successfully adapted the EQUIP program to serve adult offenders. Bud is also self-employed as a consultant to correctional and educational agencies. He retired from the Ohio Department of Youth Services in 1998, after 30 years of experience within institutions and the parole divisions. While self-employed, he has worked with agencies in 21 of the United States and 2 states in Australia. He is the past president of the Ohio Correctional and Court Services Association. Much of his professional experience has involved the use of a peer-group modality.

Beth Spring, M.A. (Virginia Tech, 1999), is a graduate of the Marriage and Family Therapy master's degree program at Virginia Tech and is a licensed marriage and family therapist in Virginia. At Northern Virginia Family Services, she works as a counselor for families and youths. She has made critical contributions to *EQUIP for Educators*, including development of The Millionaire Game described in chapter 2. She has worked for 20 years as a journalist and editor. For several years before becoming a therapist, she worked as a contract editor for the Child Welfare League of America, editing training materials. Currently, she works at Northern Virginia Family Service, in Oakton, and has a private practice in Vienna, Virginia.